She Was a Hairy Bear,

She Was a Scary Bear

Words and art by

Louisa Bermingham

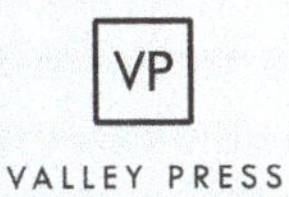

VALLEY PRESS

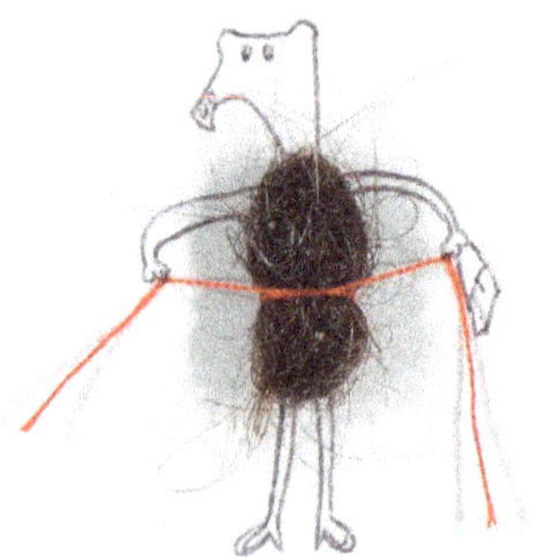

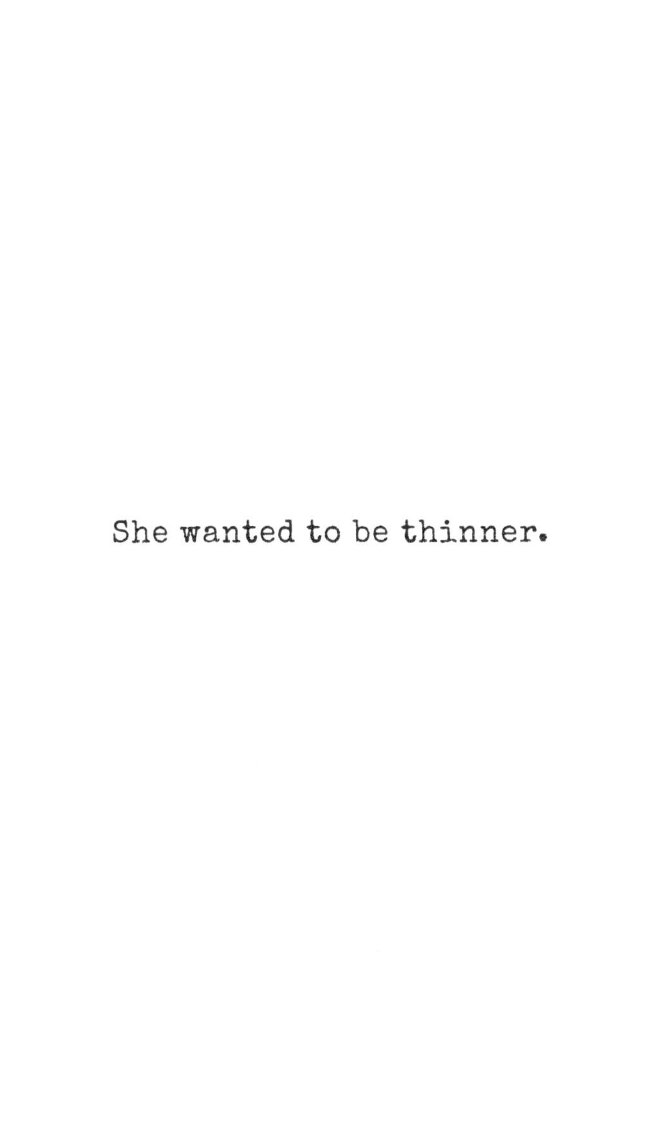

She wanted to be thinner.

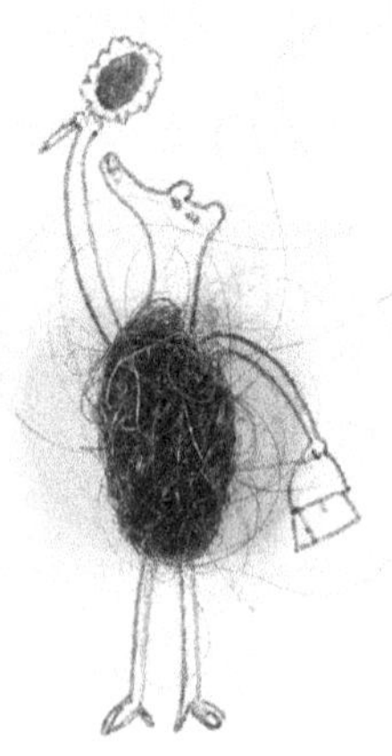

She found a grey hair.

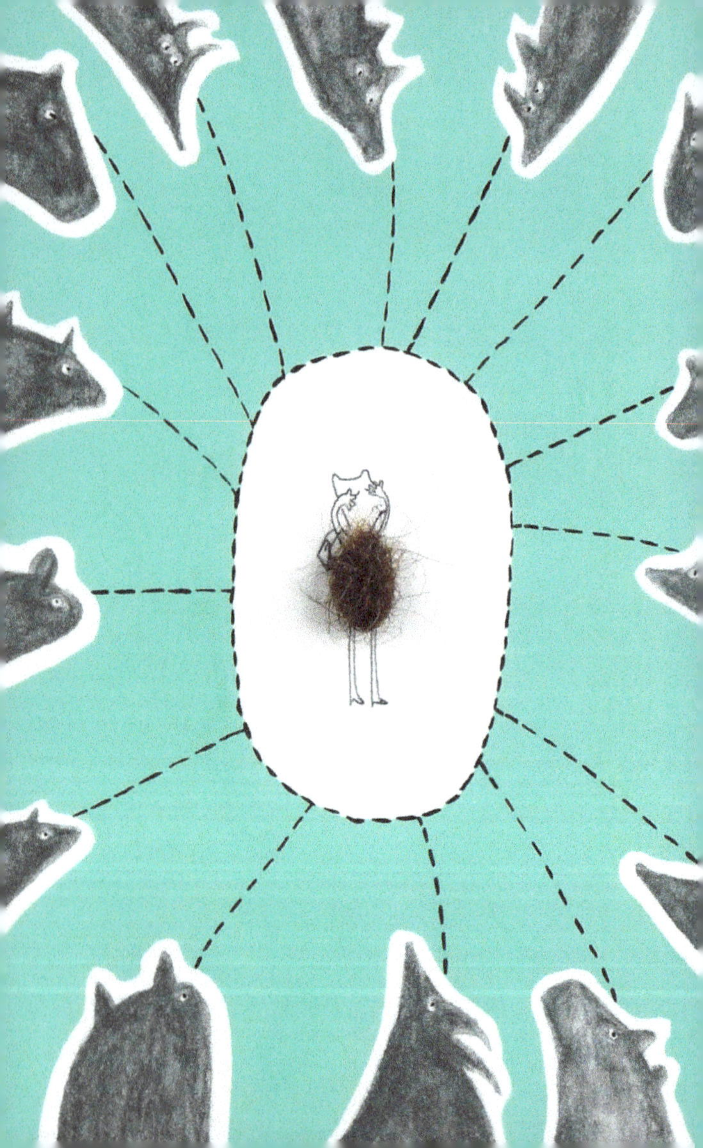

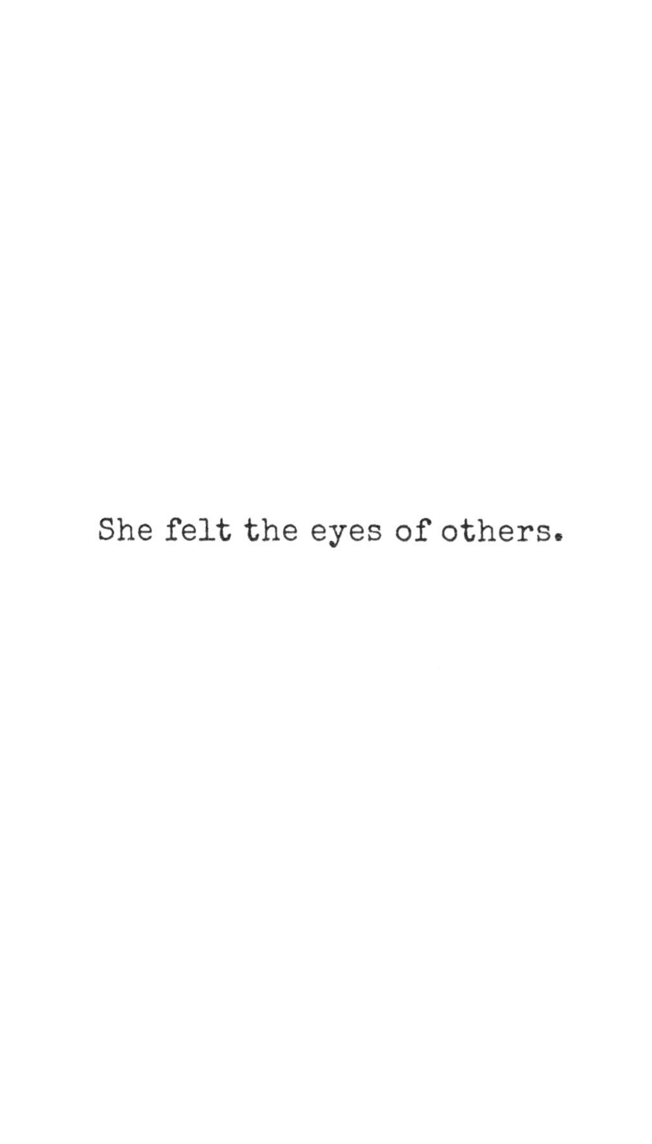

She felt the eyes of others.

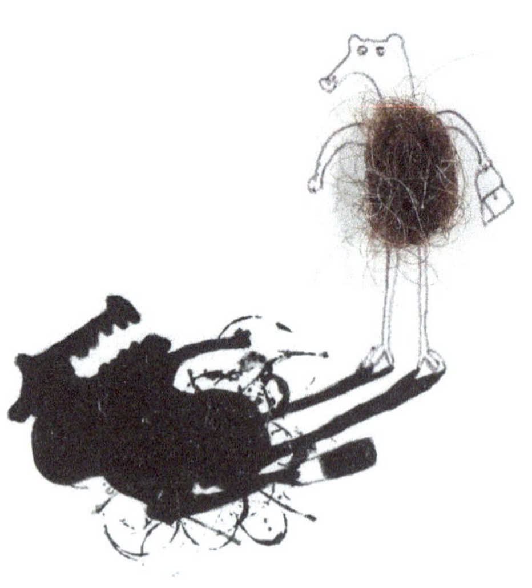

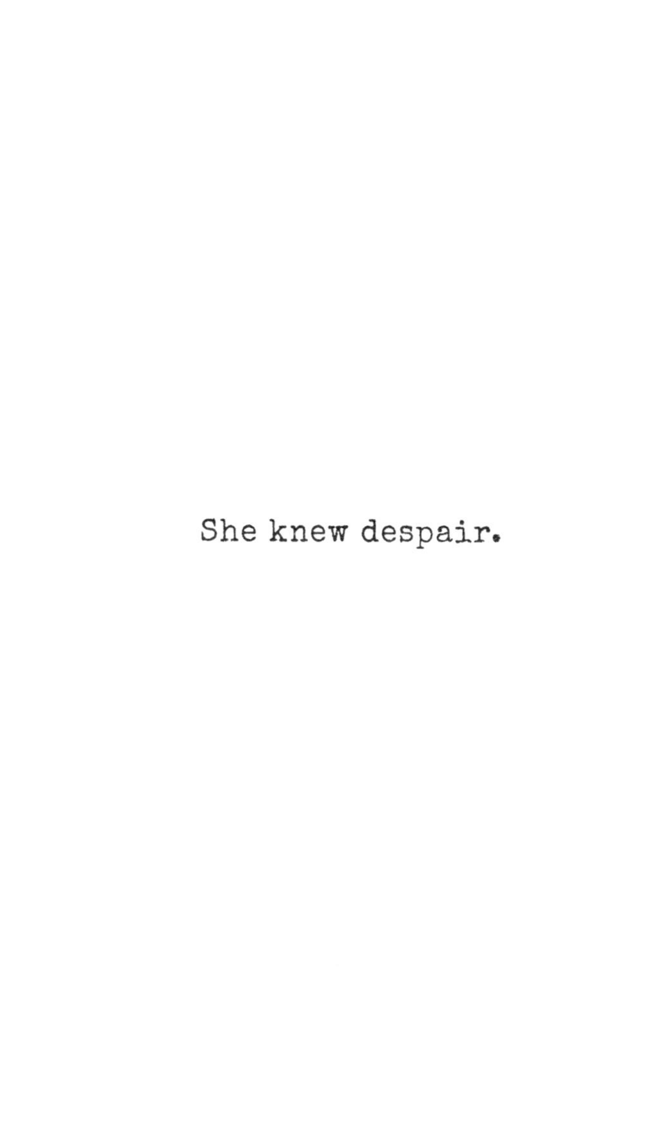
She knew despair.

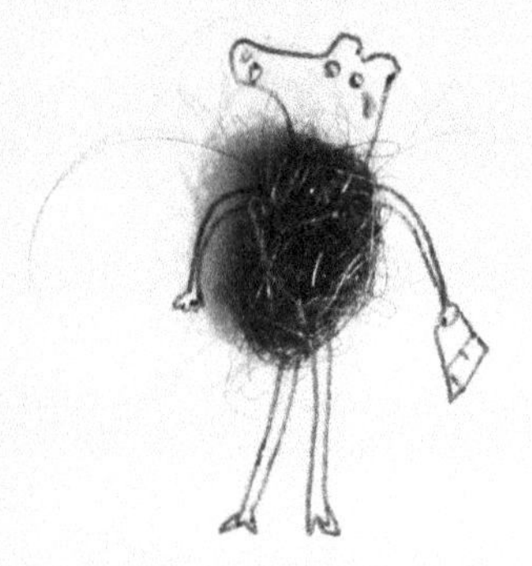

She cried.

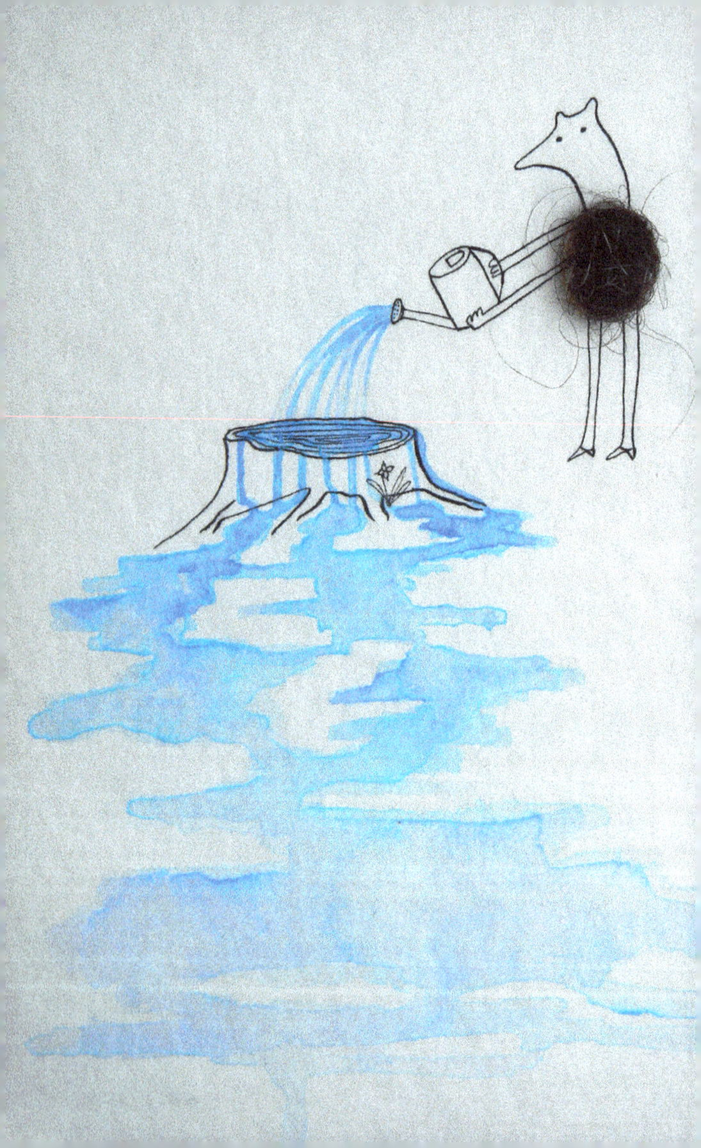

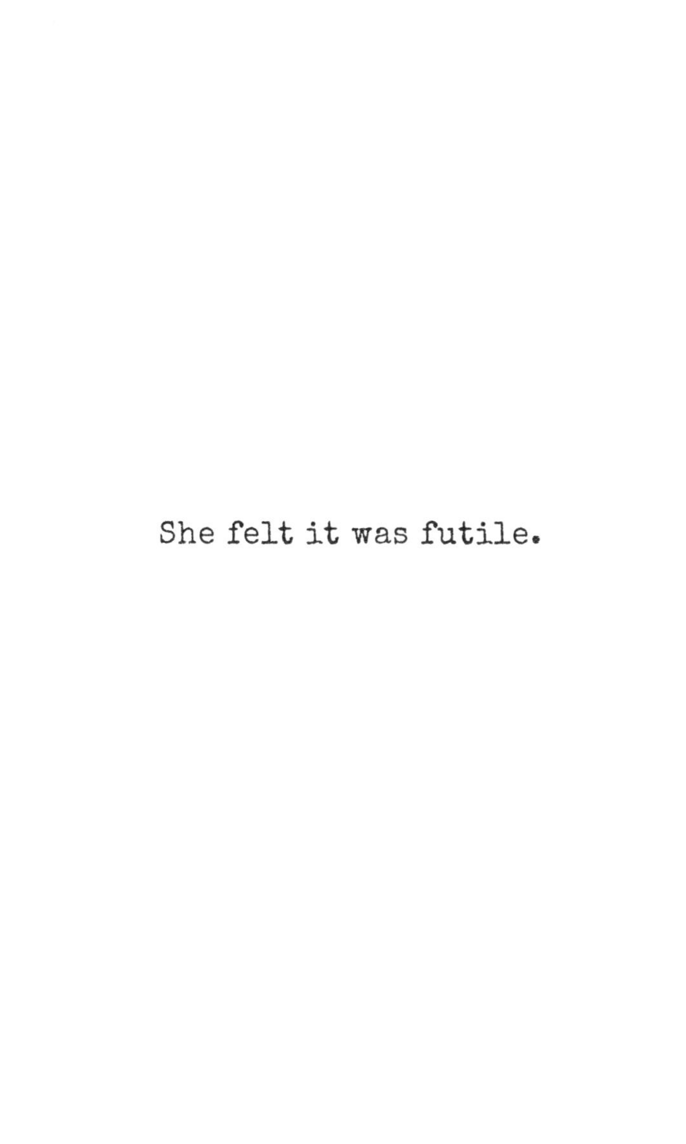

She felt it was futile.

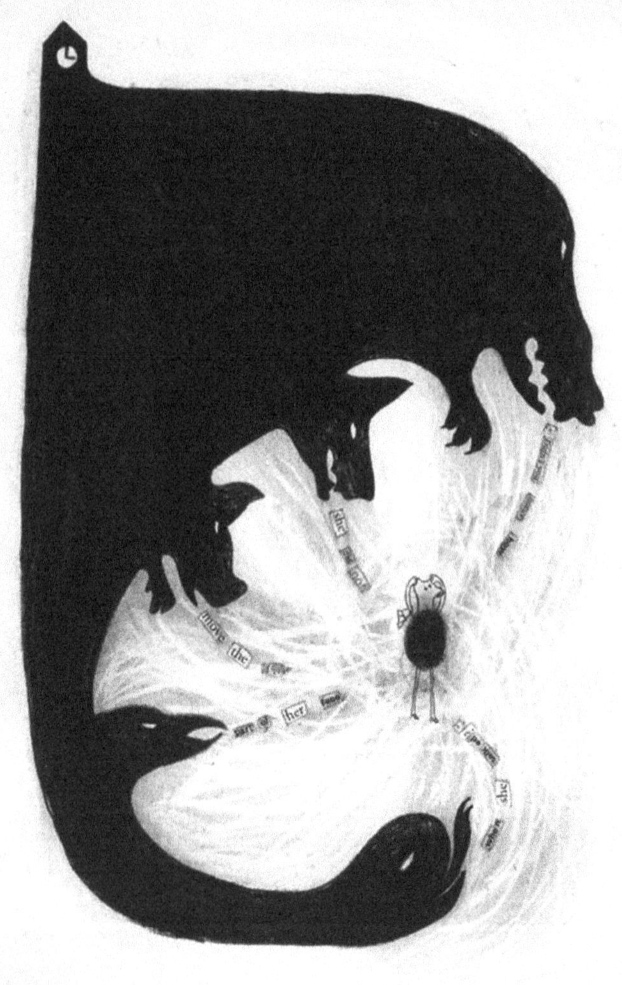
she
more the
her
she

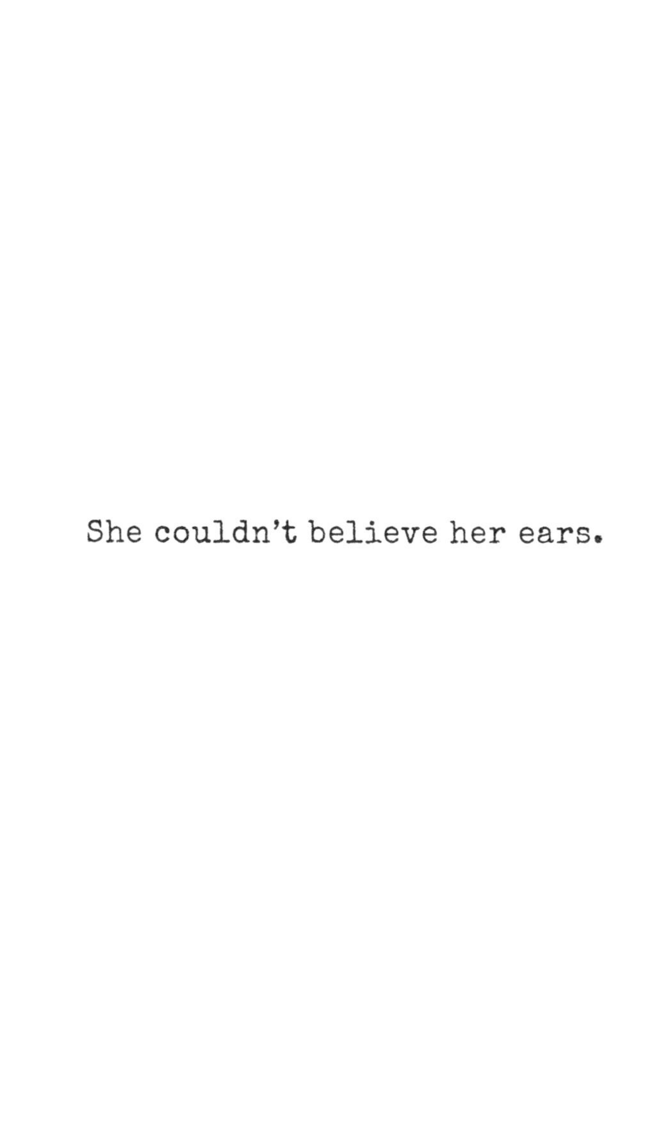

She couldn't believe her ears.

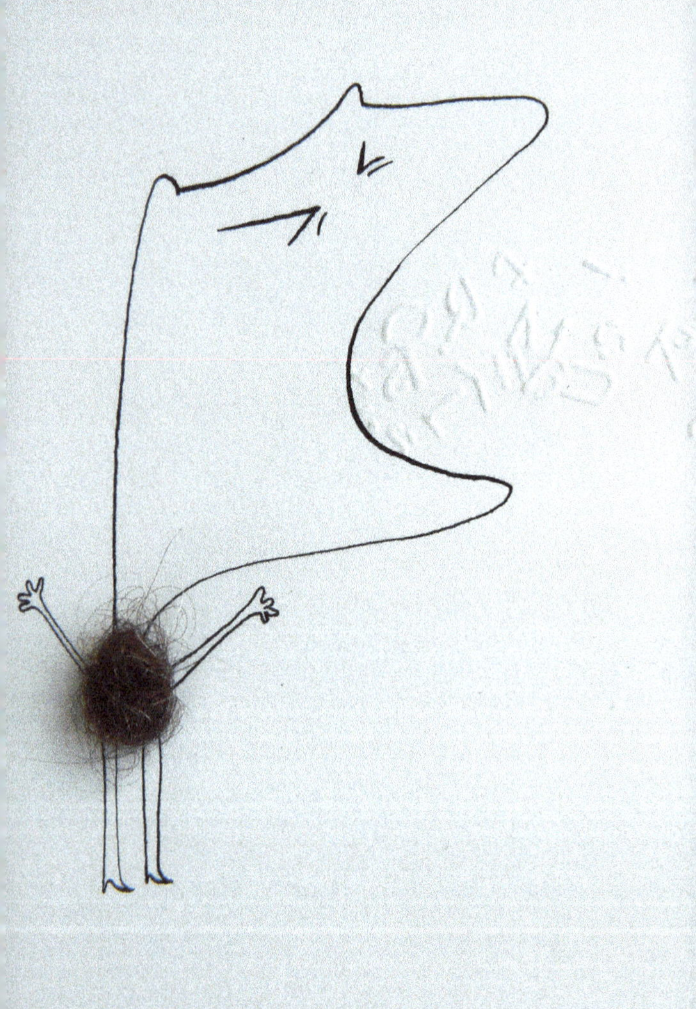

She wasn't heard.

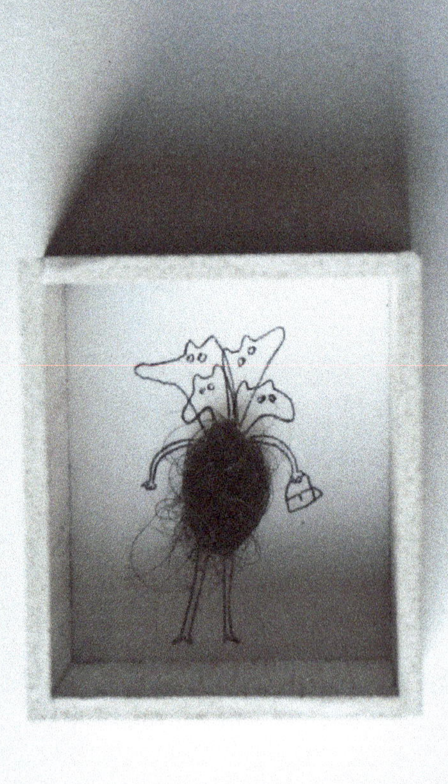

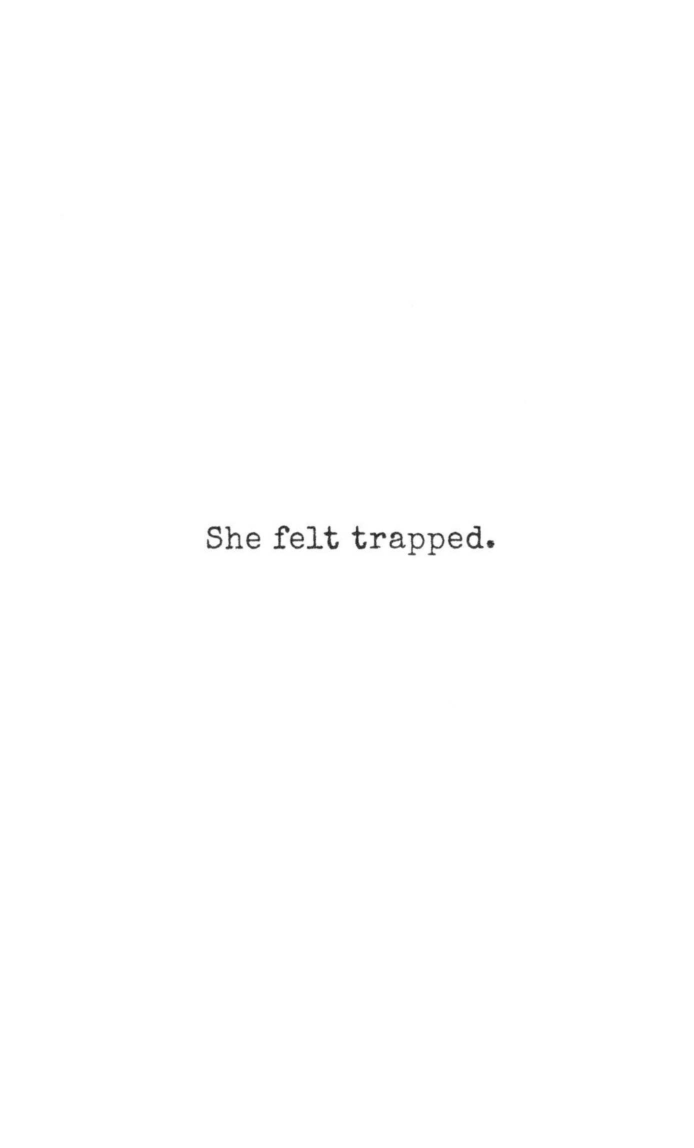

She felt trapped.

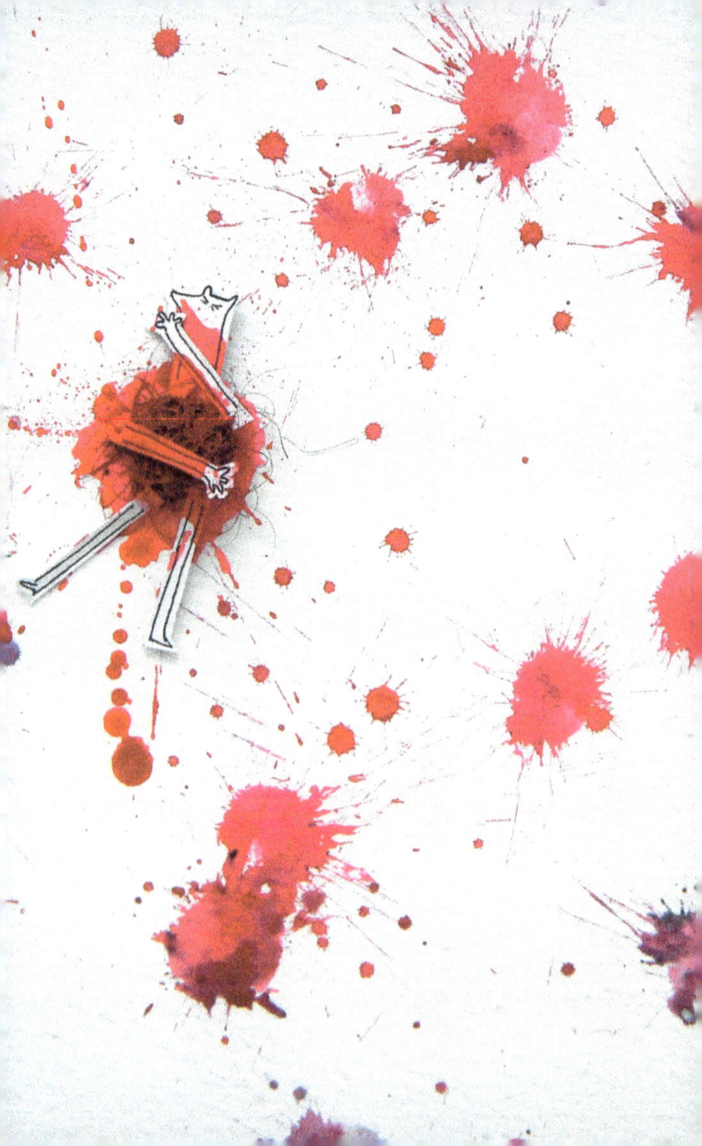

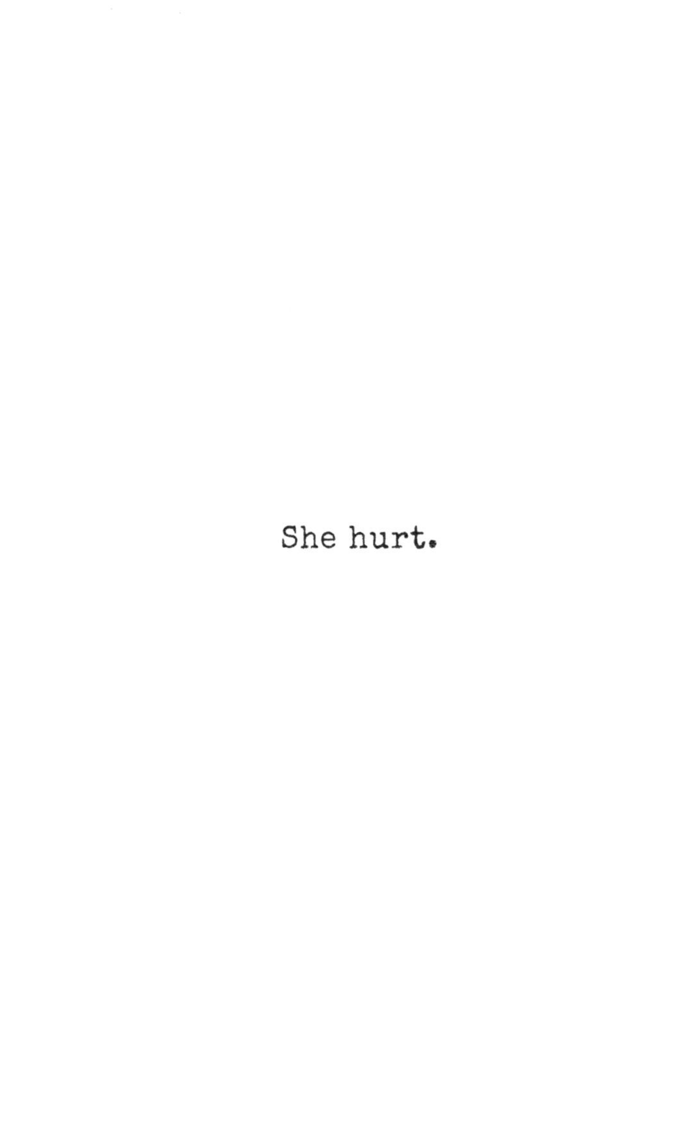

She hurt.

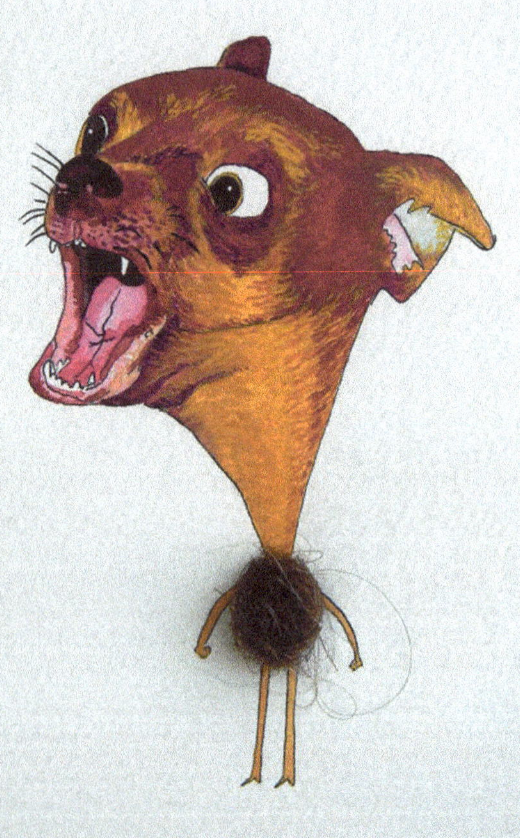

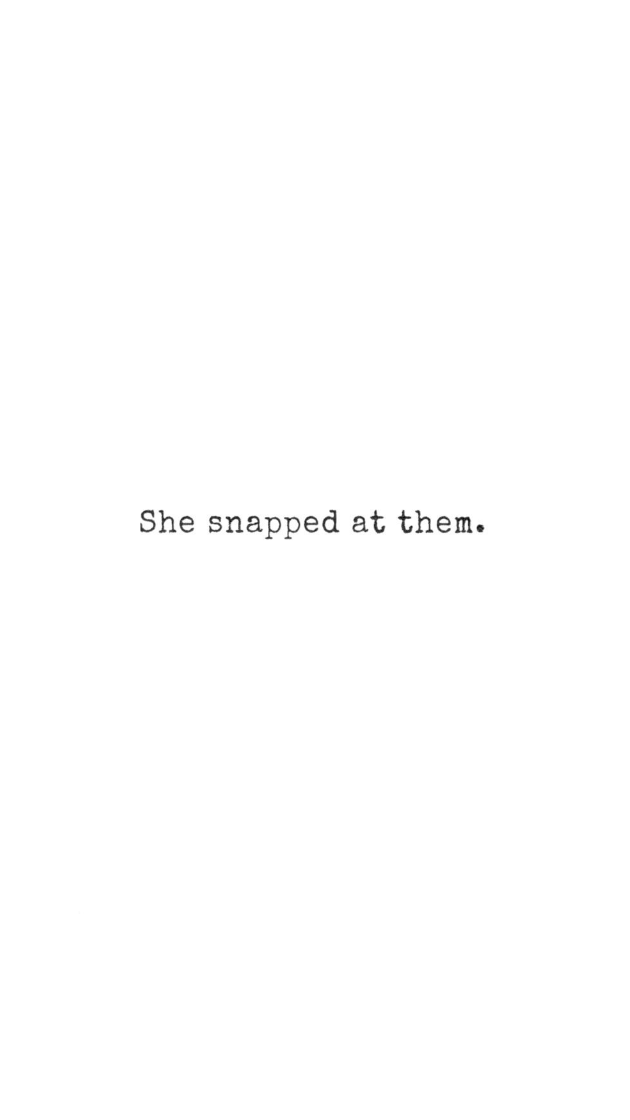

She snapped at them.

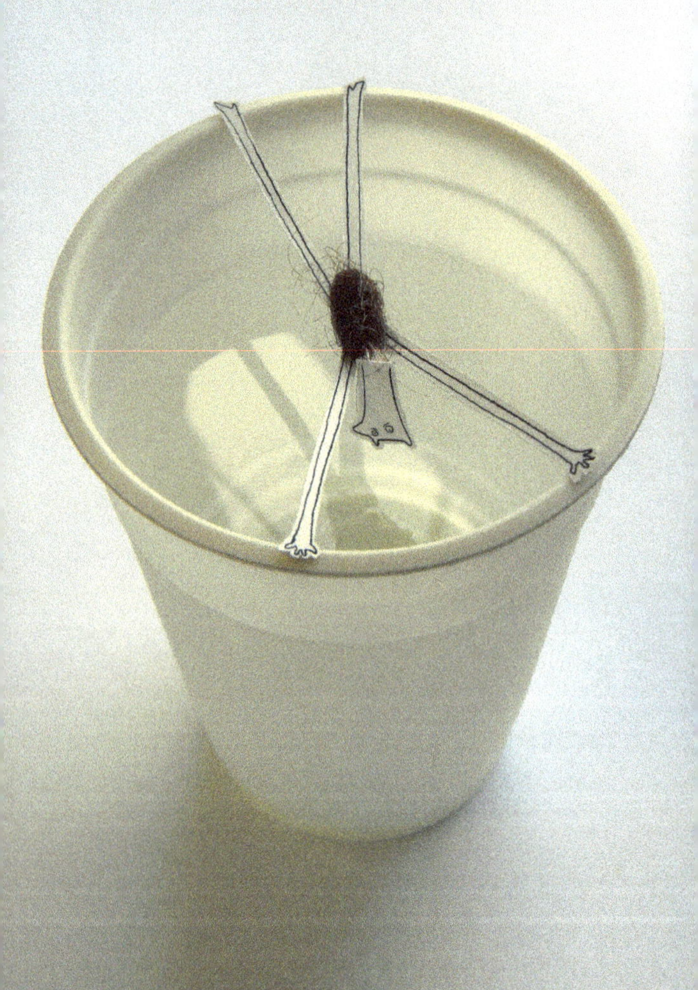

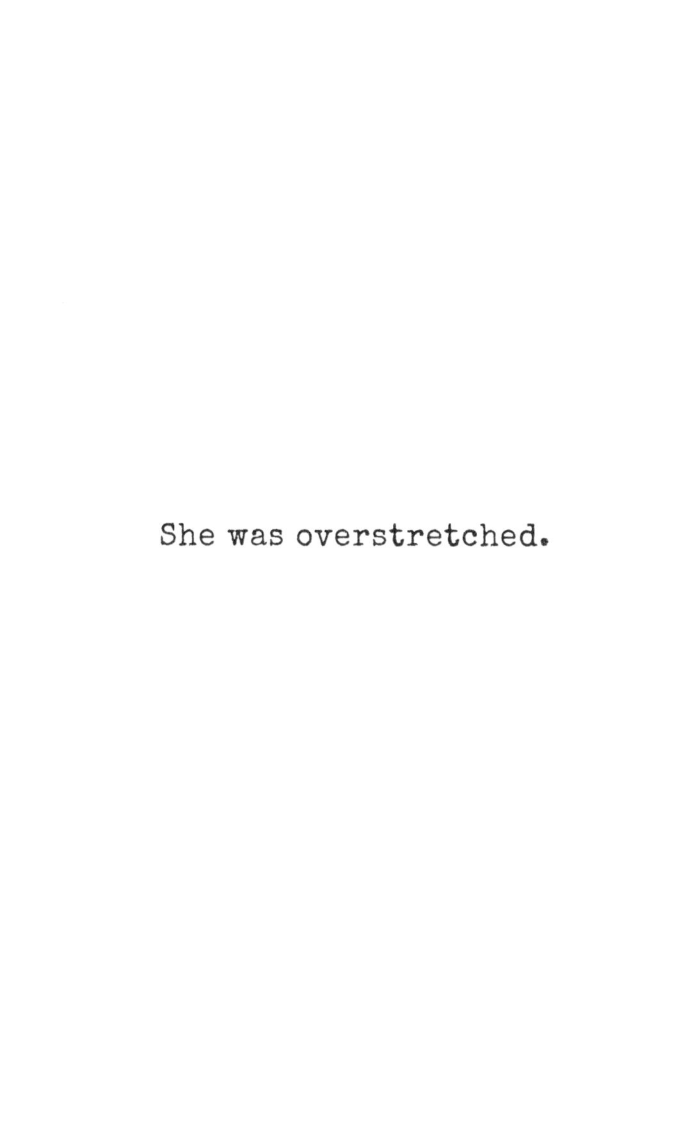

She was overstretched.

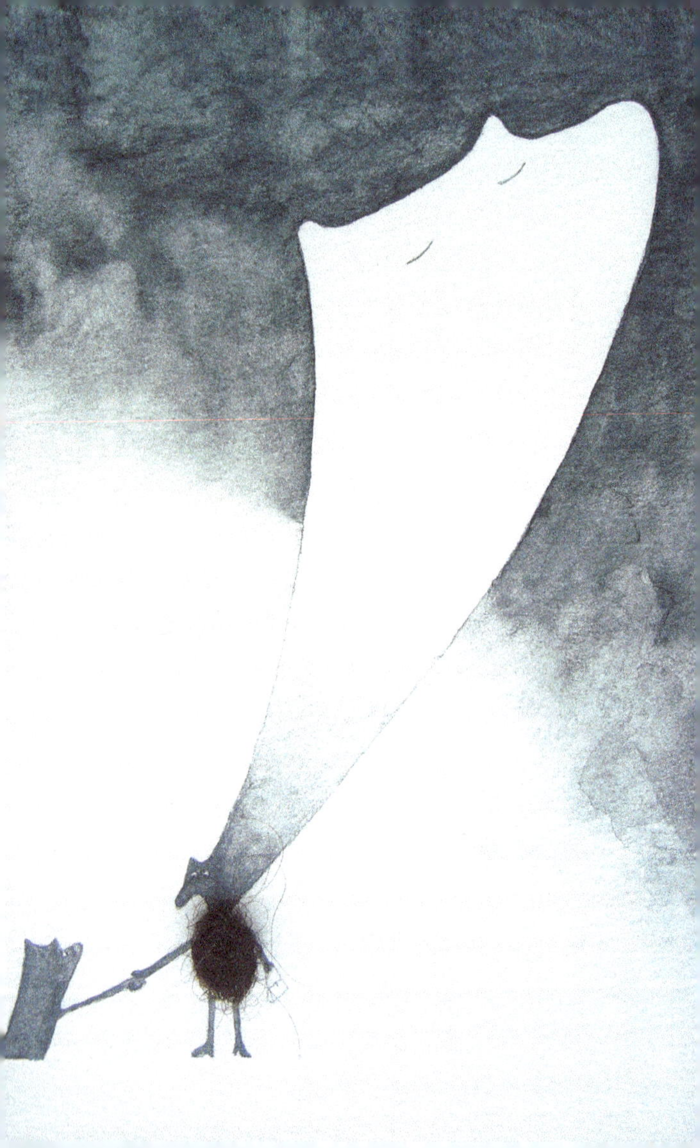

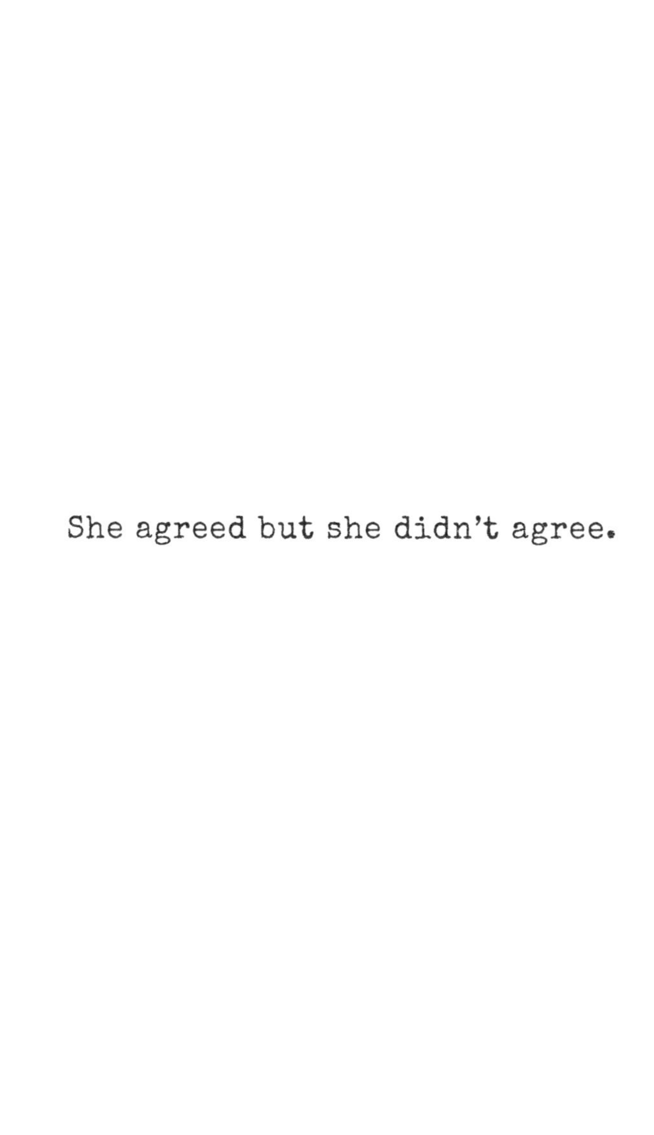

She agreed but she didn't agree.

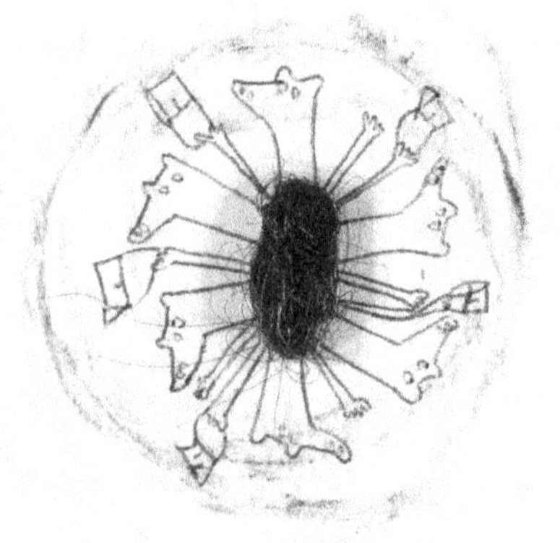

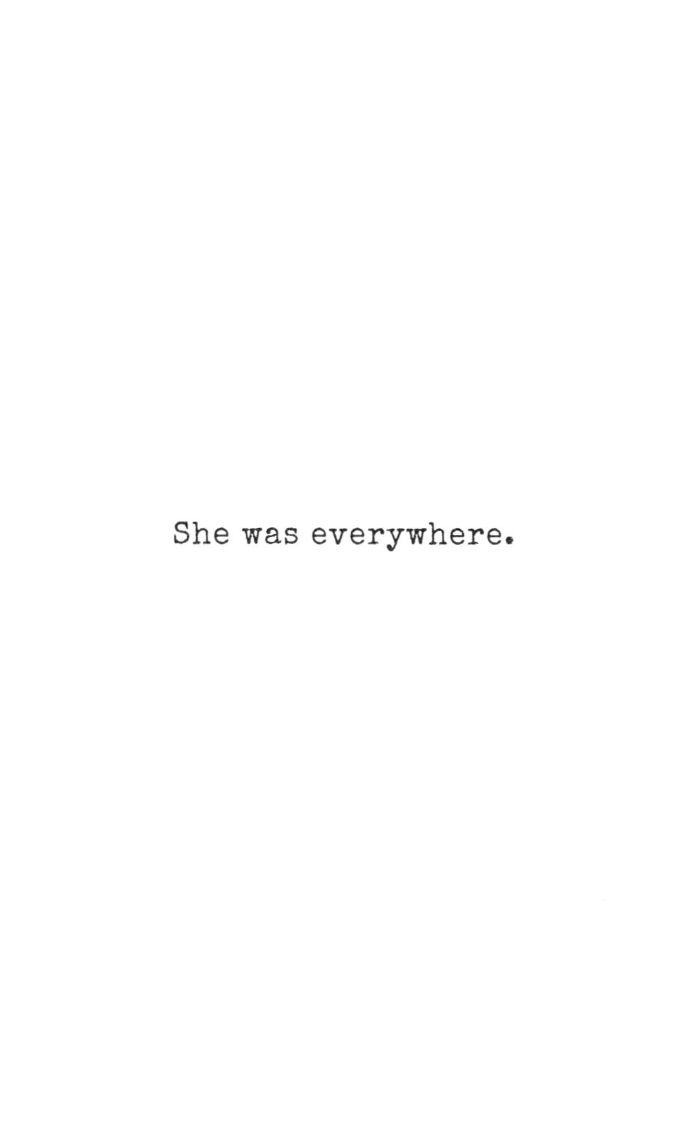

She was everywhere.

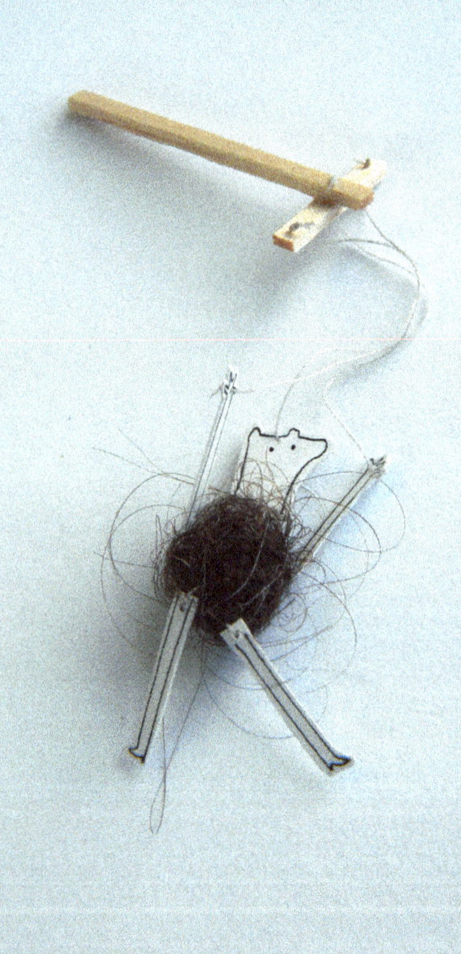

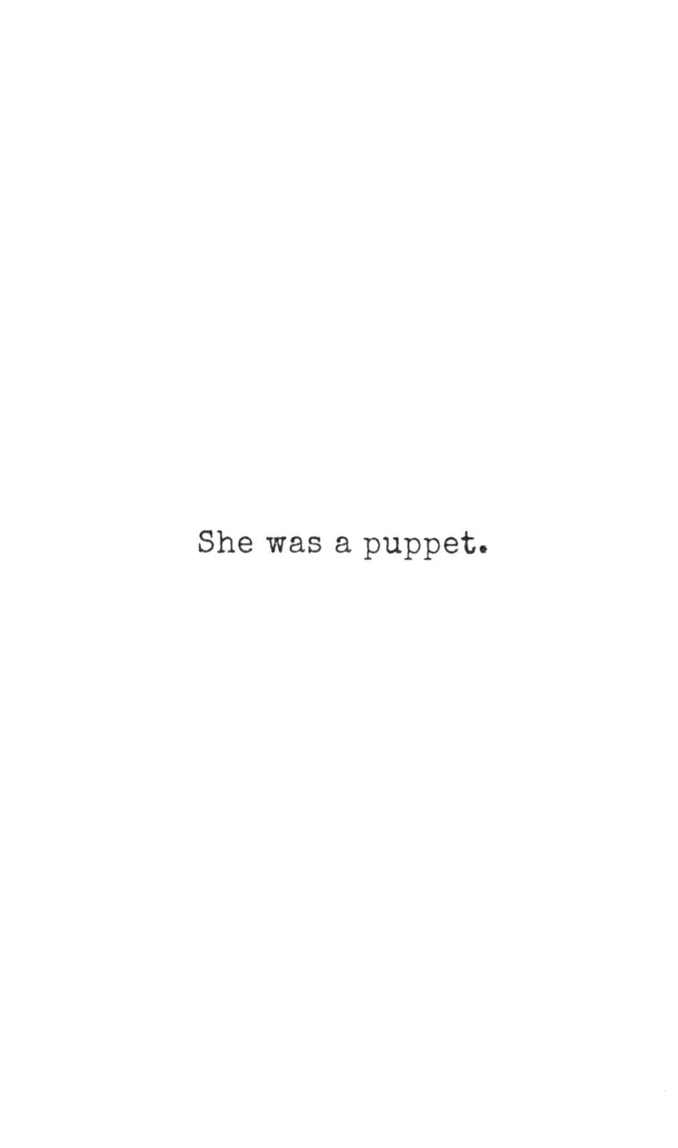

She was a puppet.

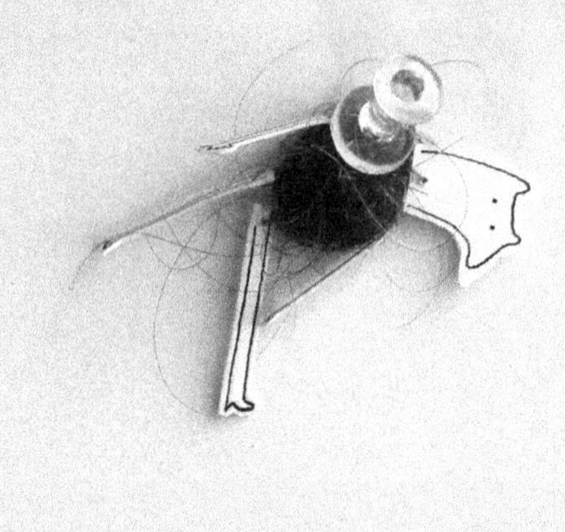

She was hung out to dry.

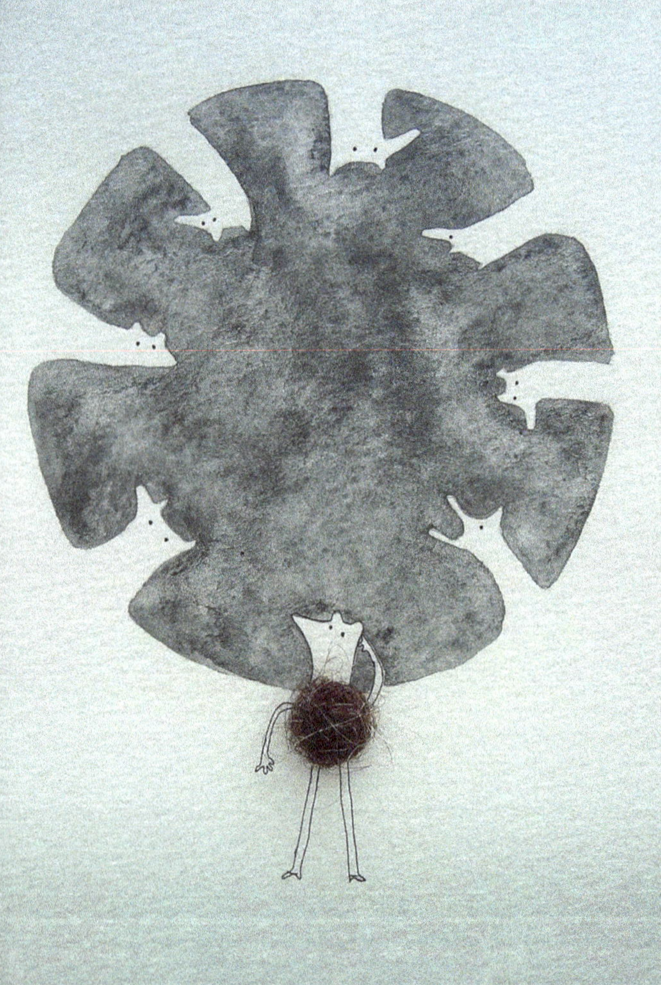

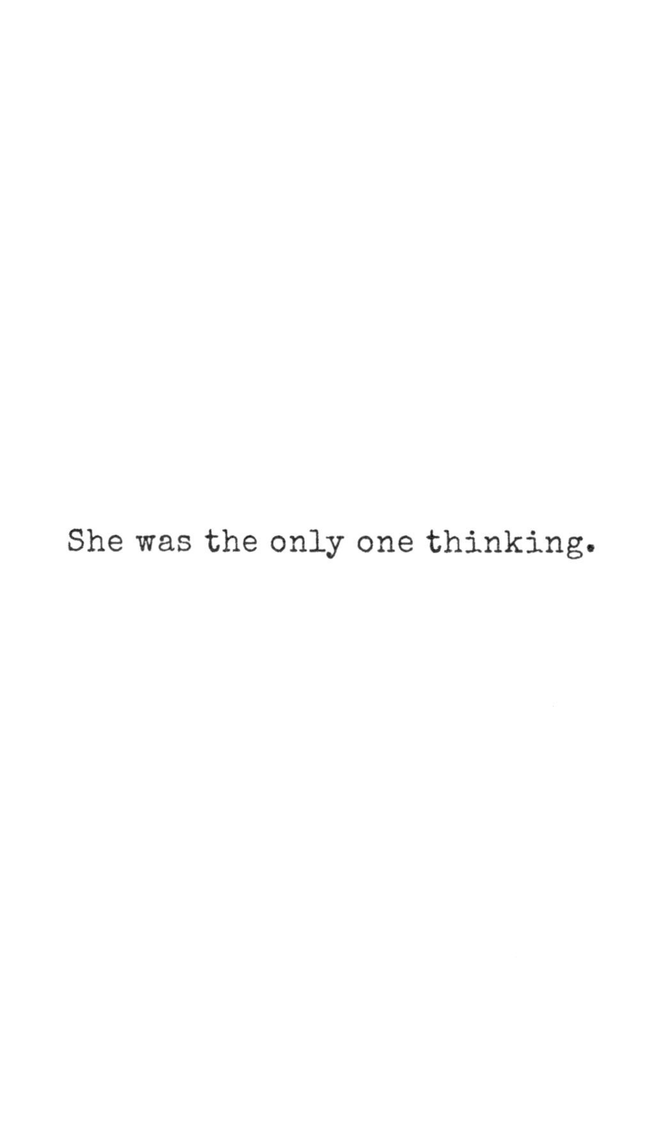

She was the only one thinking.

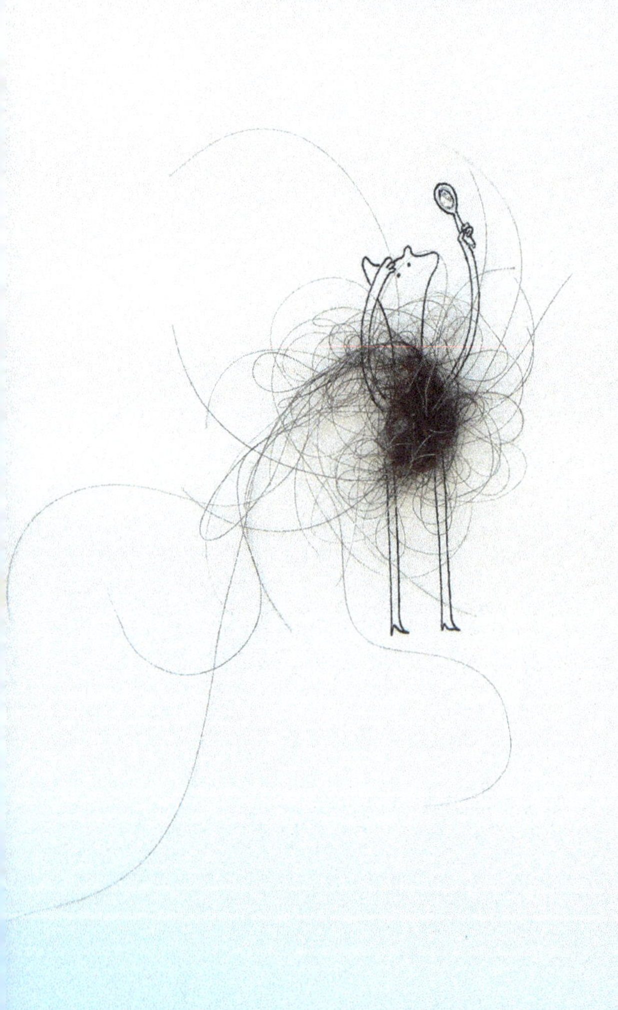

She always had a hair
out of place.

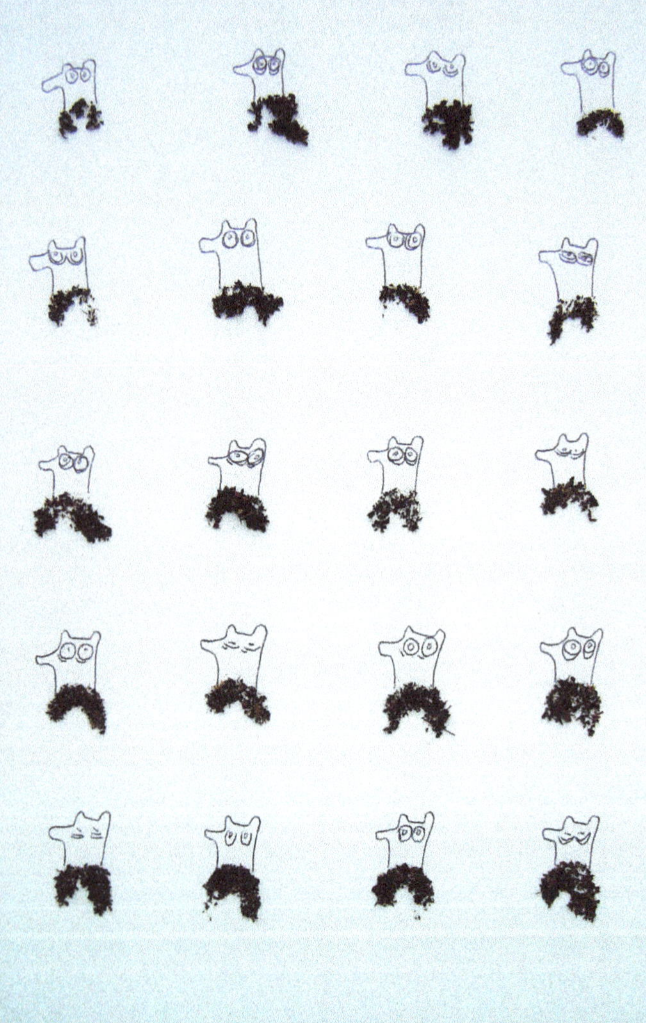

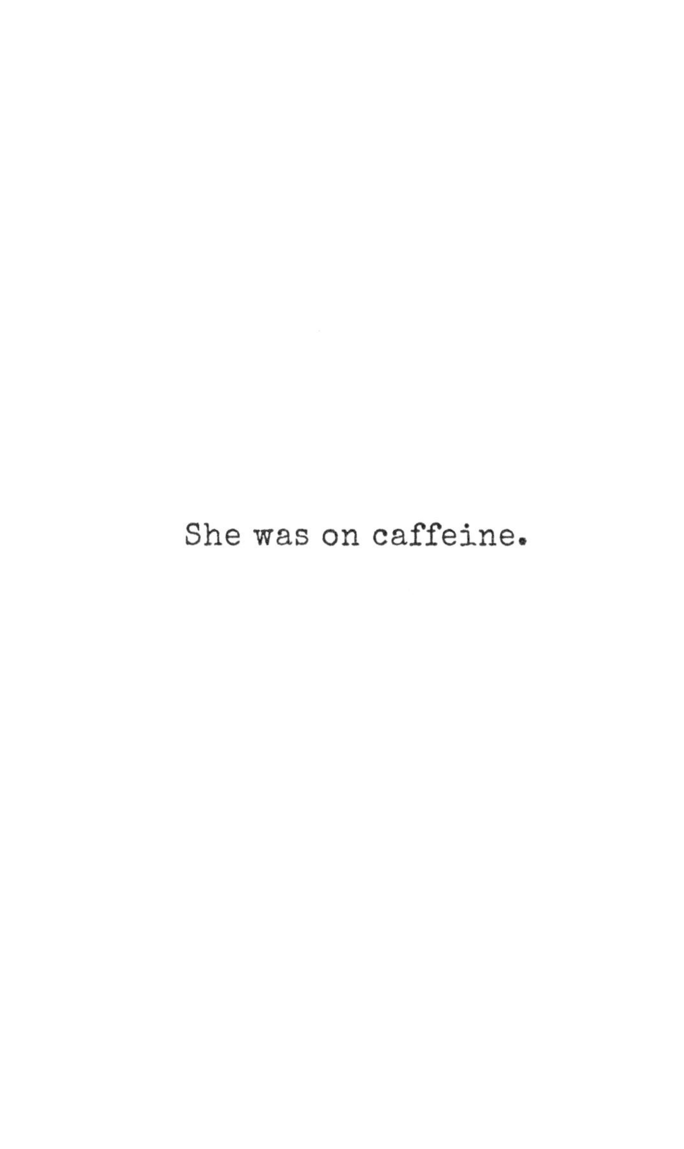

She was on caffeine.

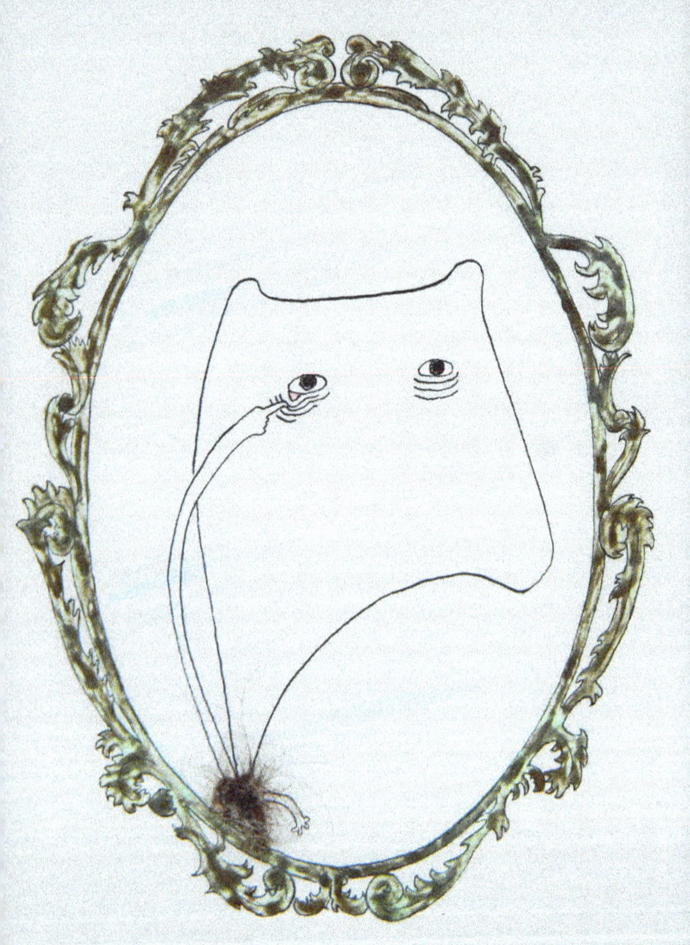

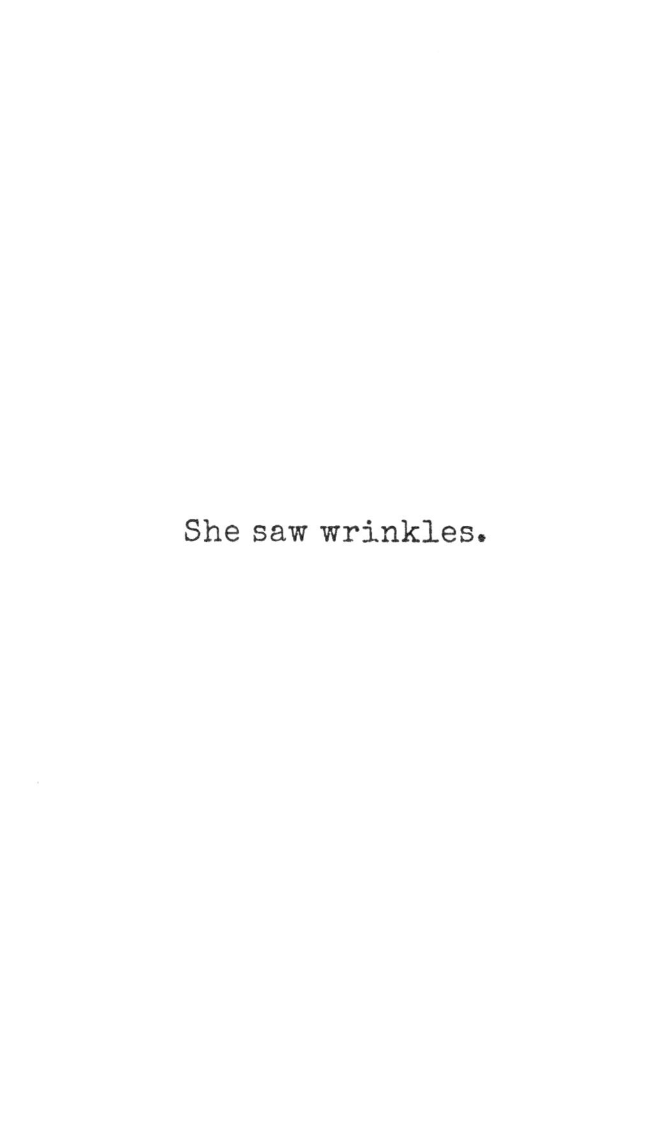

She saw wrinkles.

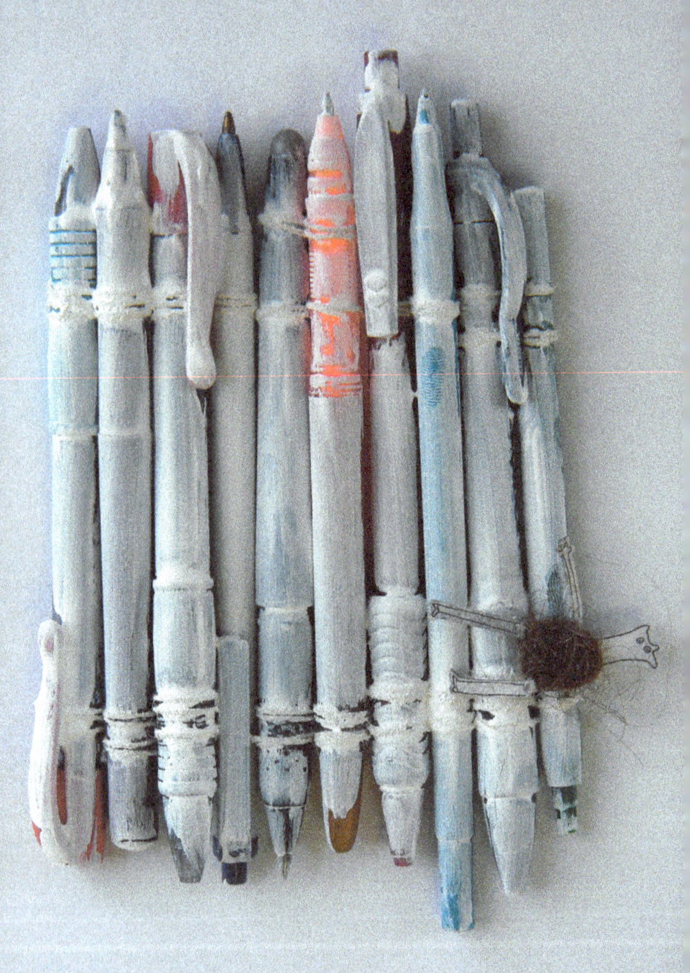

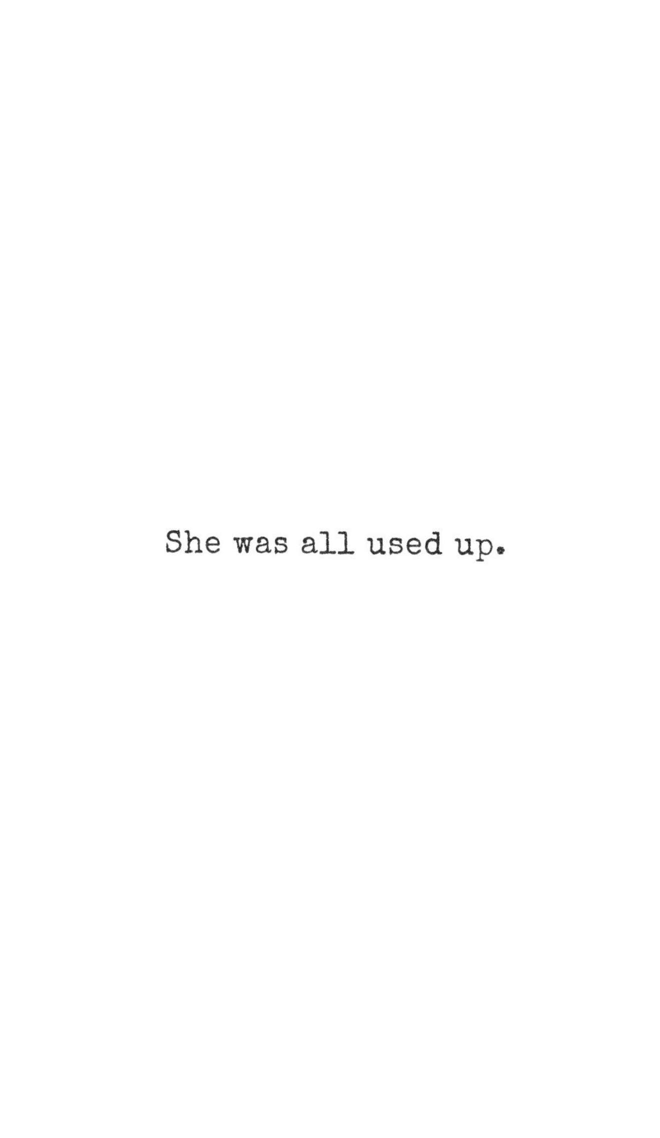
She was all used up.

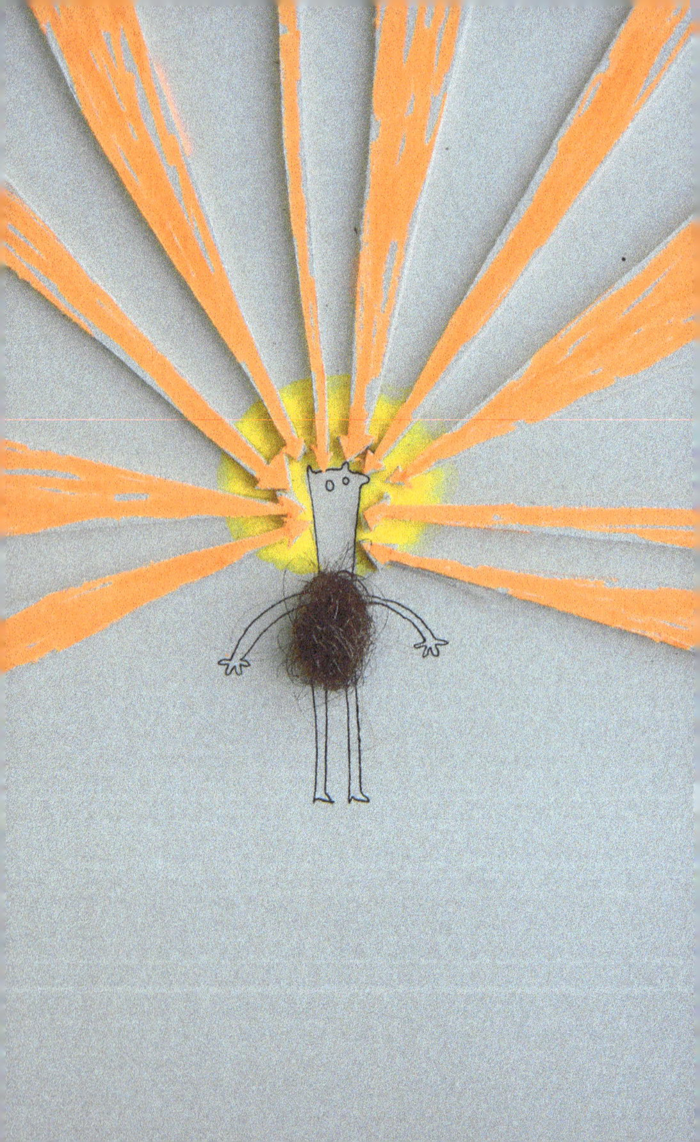

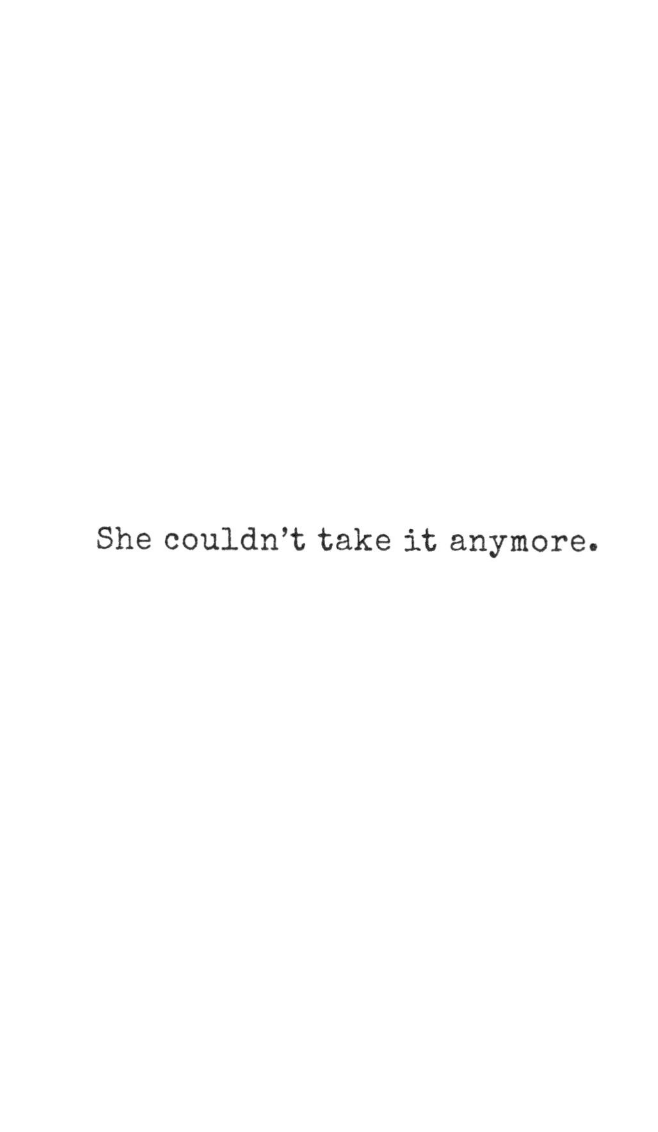
She couldn't take it anymore.

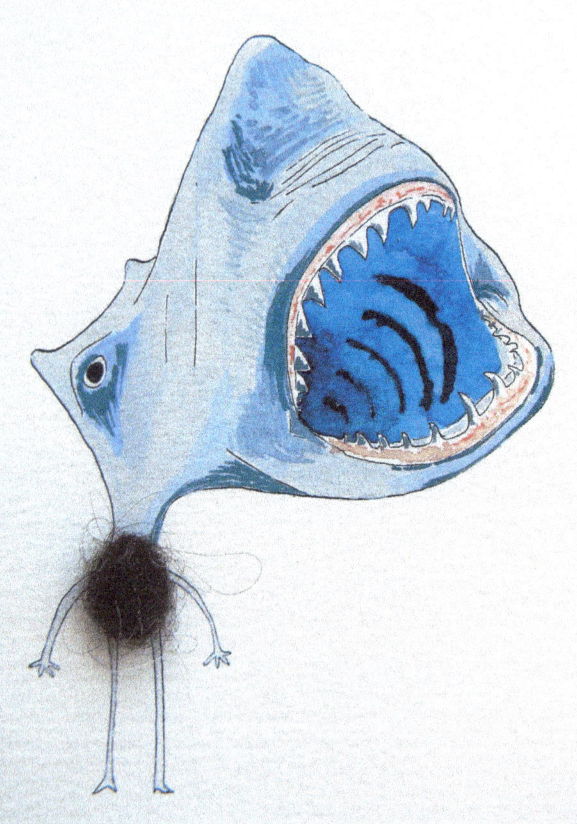

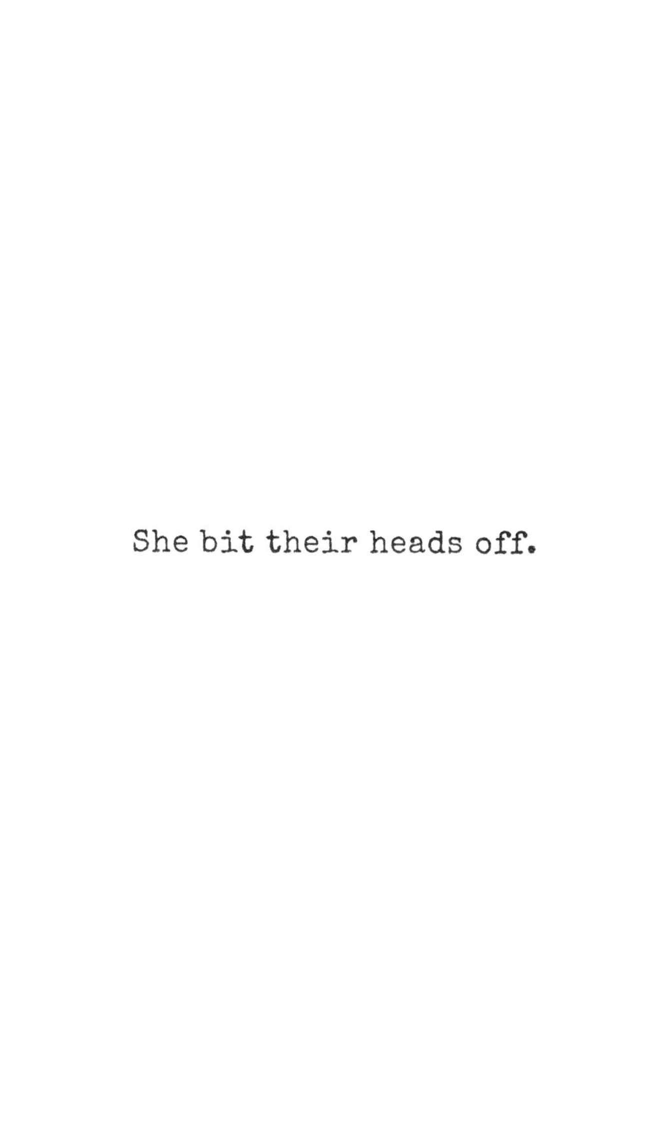
She bit their heads off.

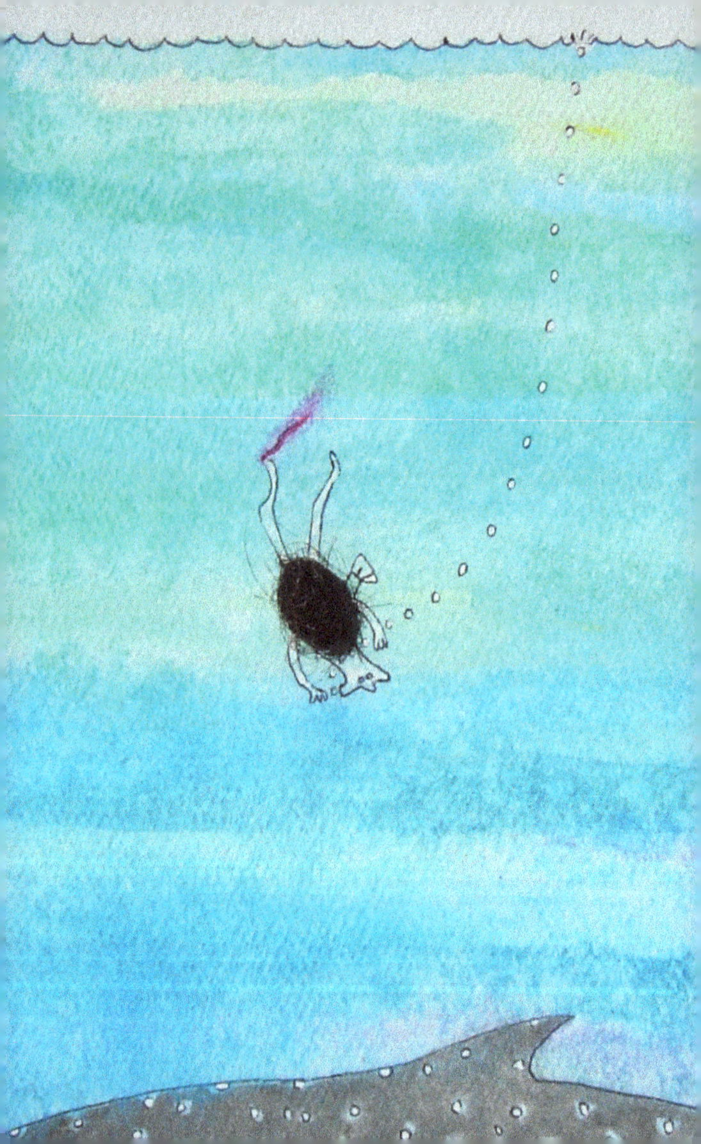

She had a puncture.

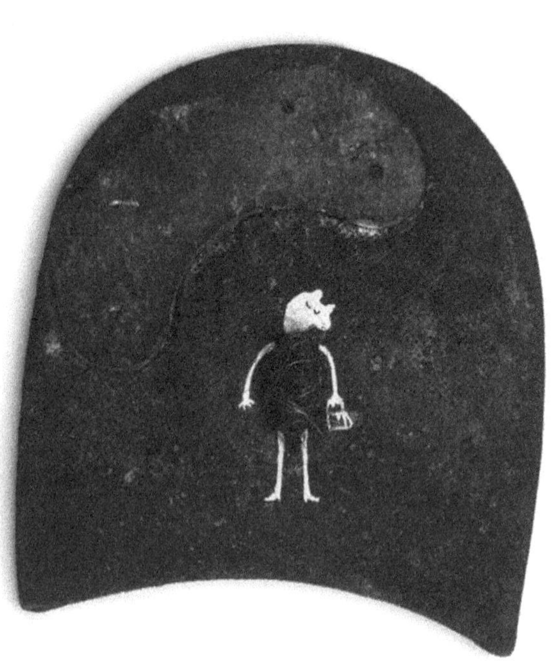

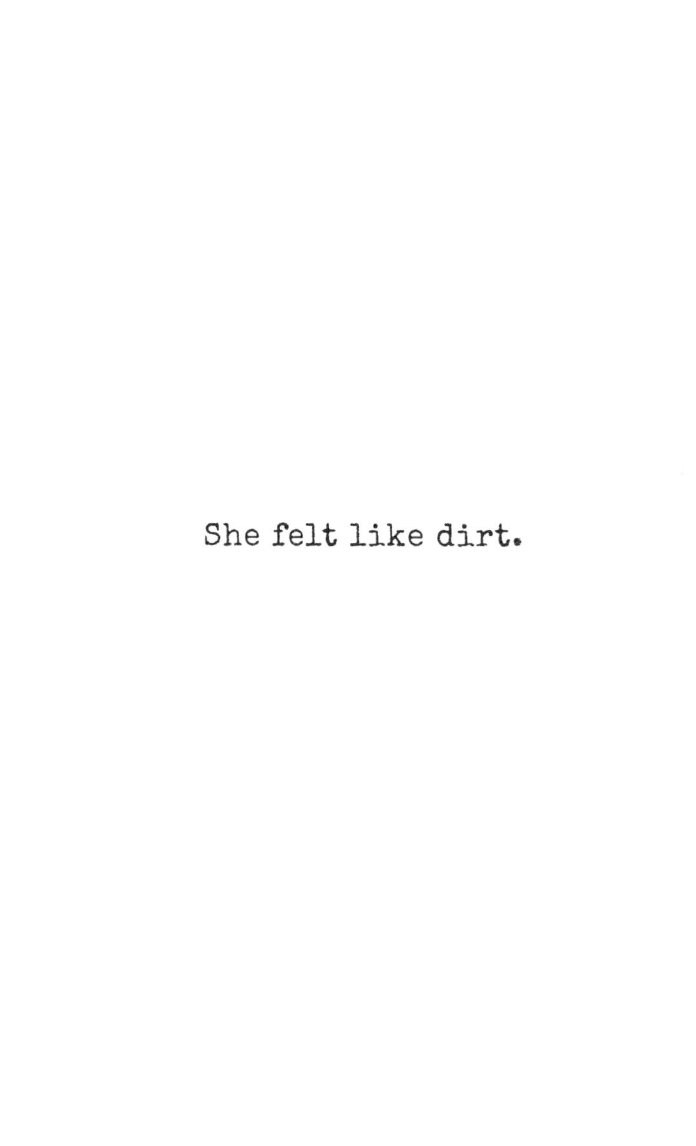

She felt like dirt.

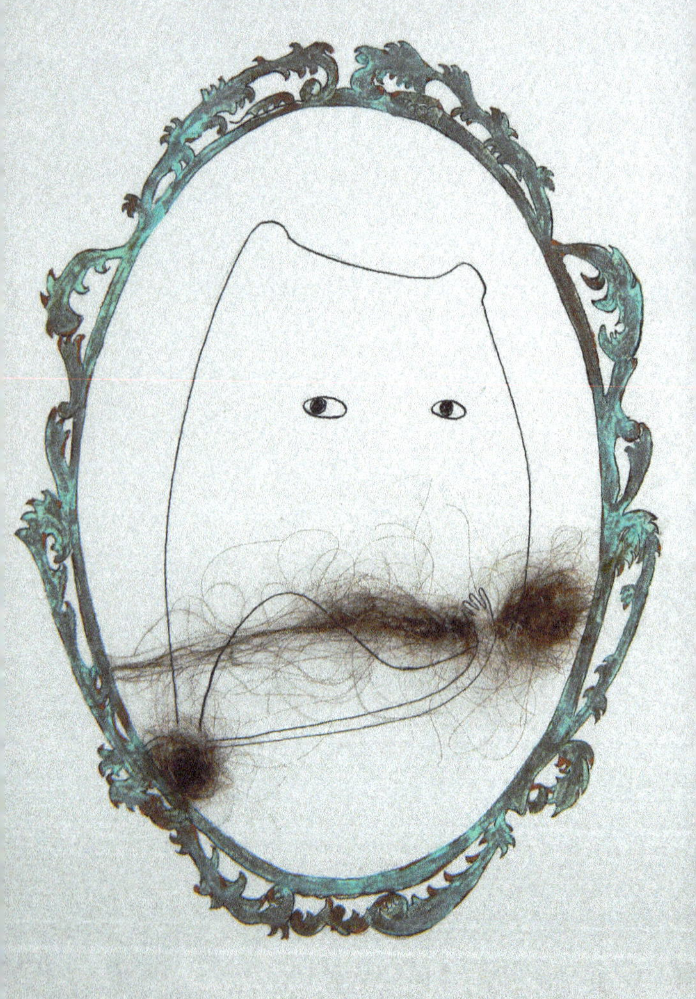

She seemed to be growing
a moustache.

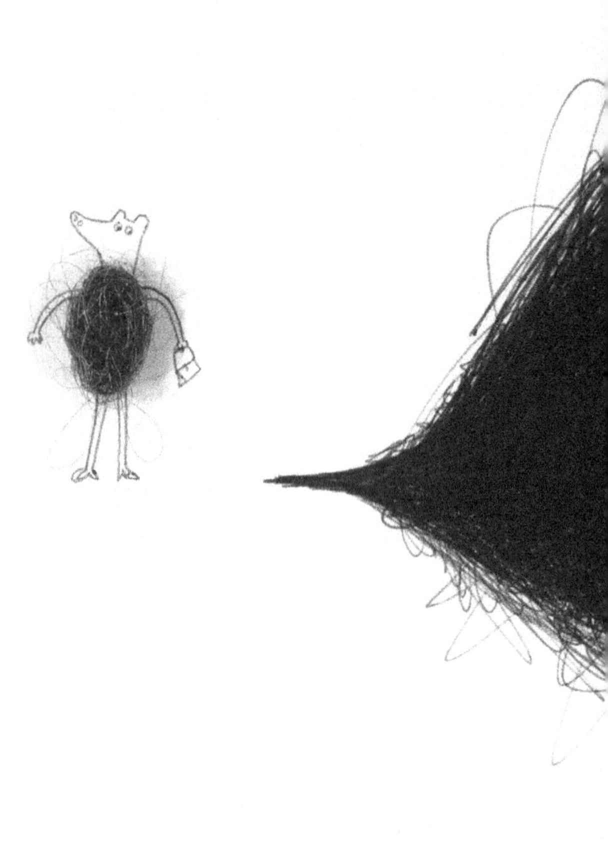

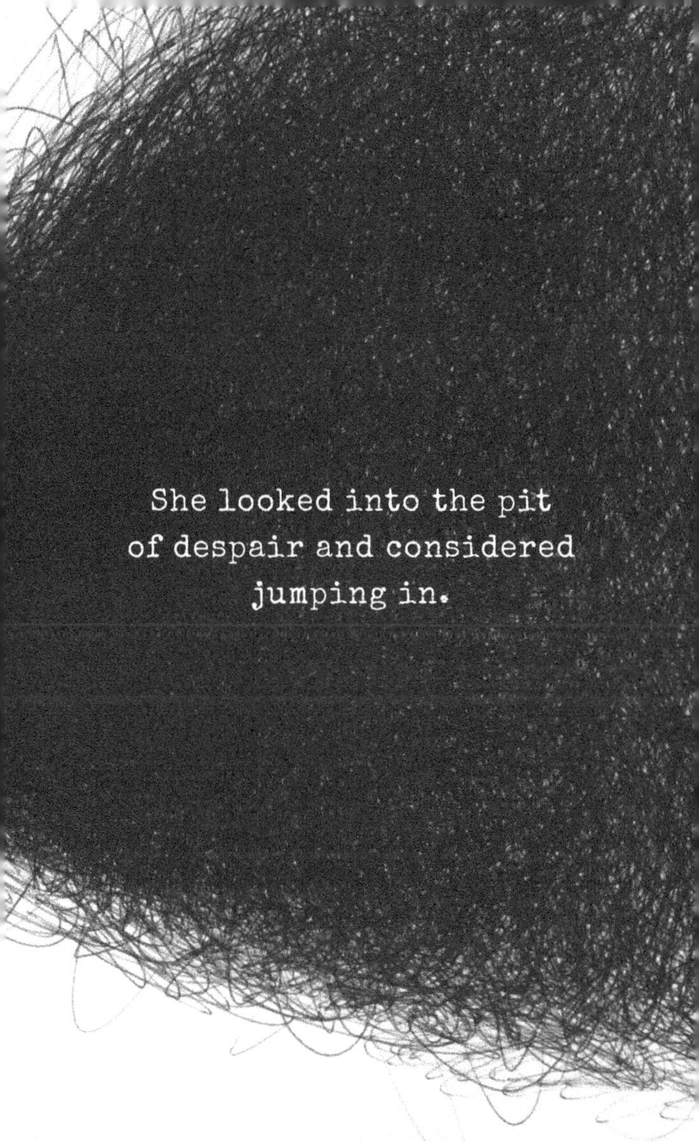
She looked into the pit
of despair and considered
jumping in.

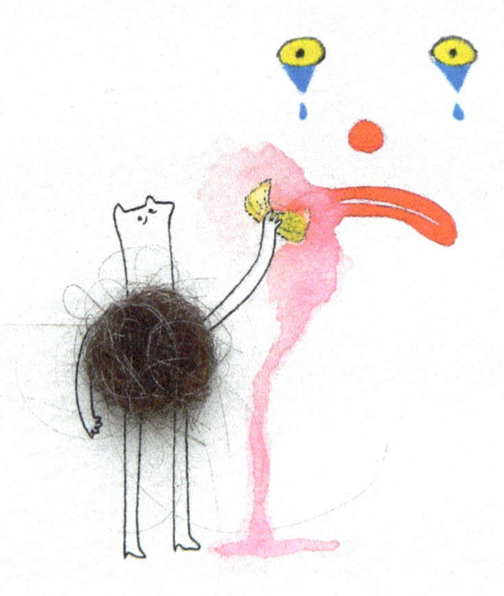

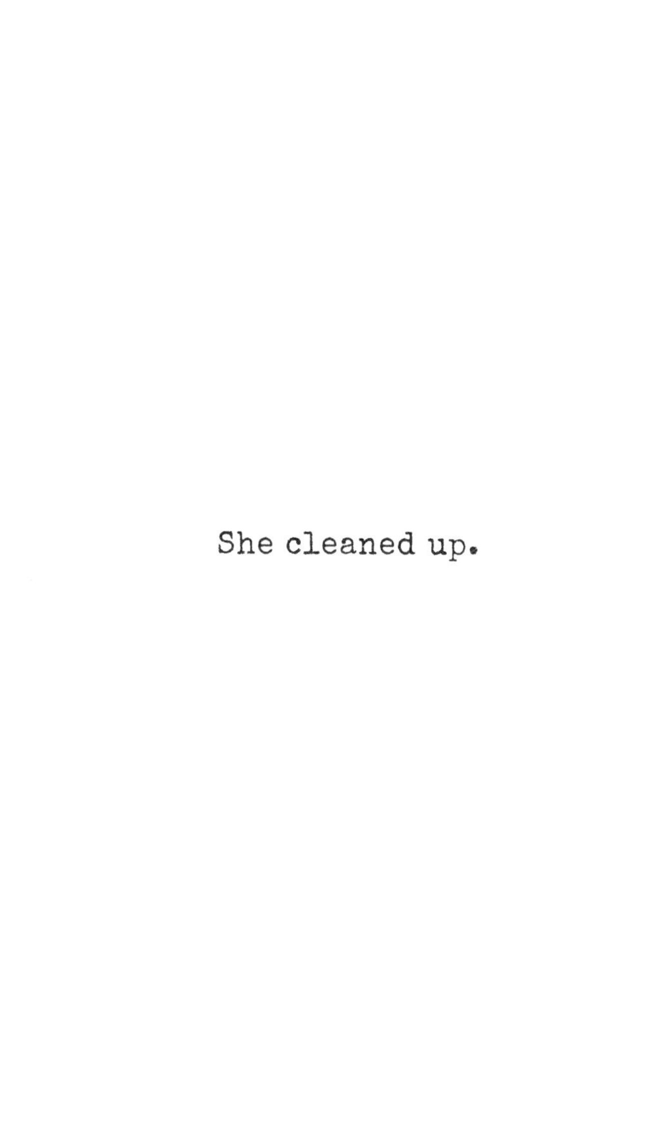

She cleaned up.

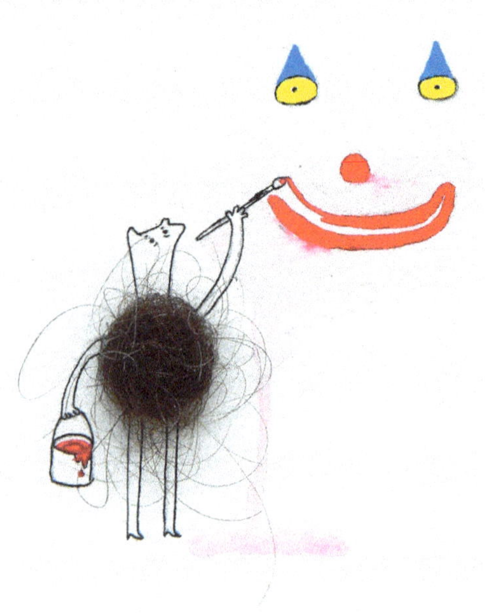

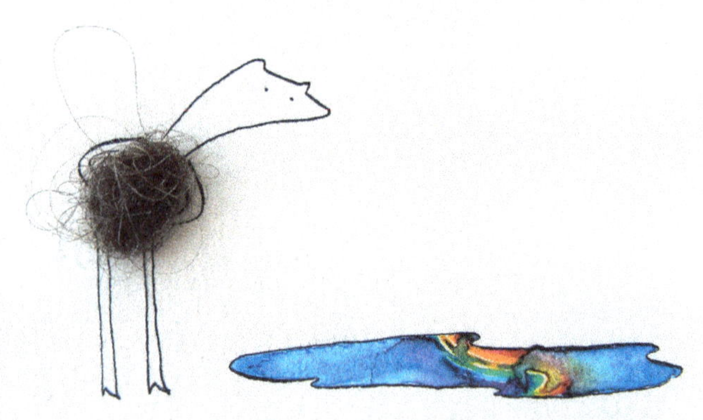

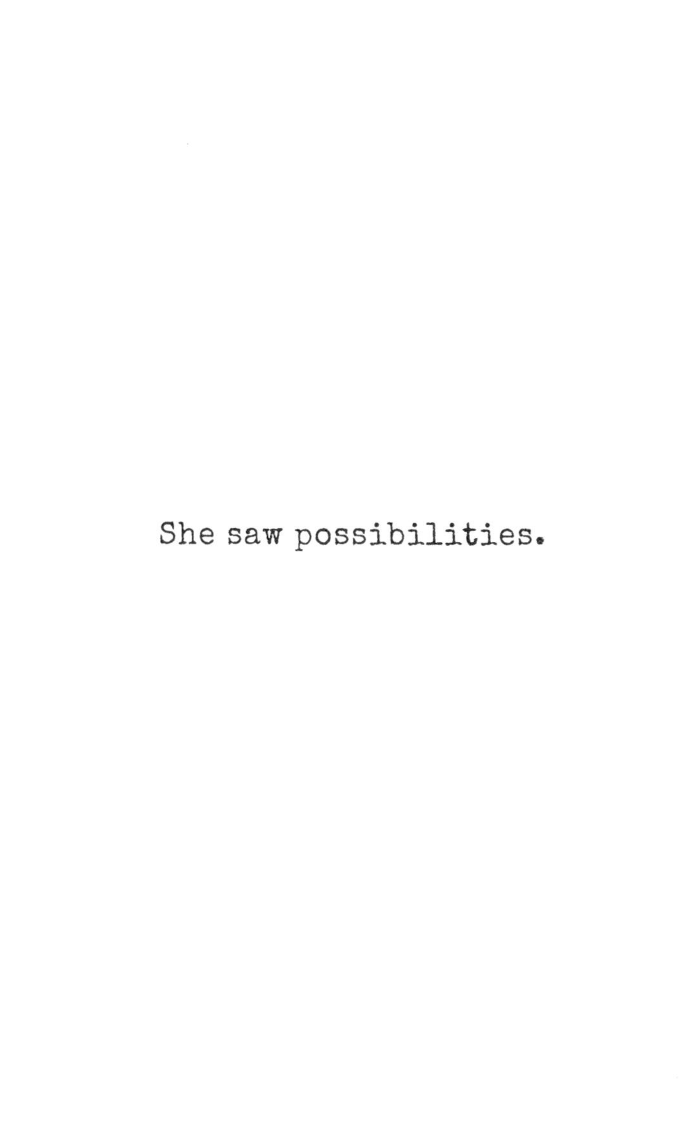

She saw possibilities.

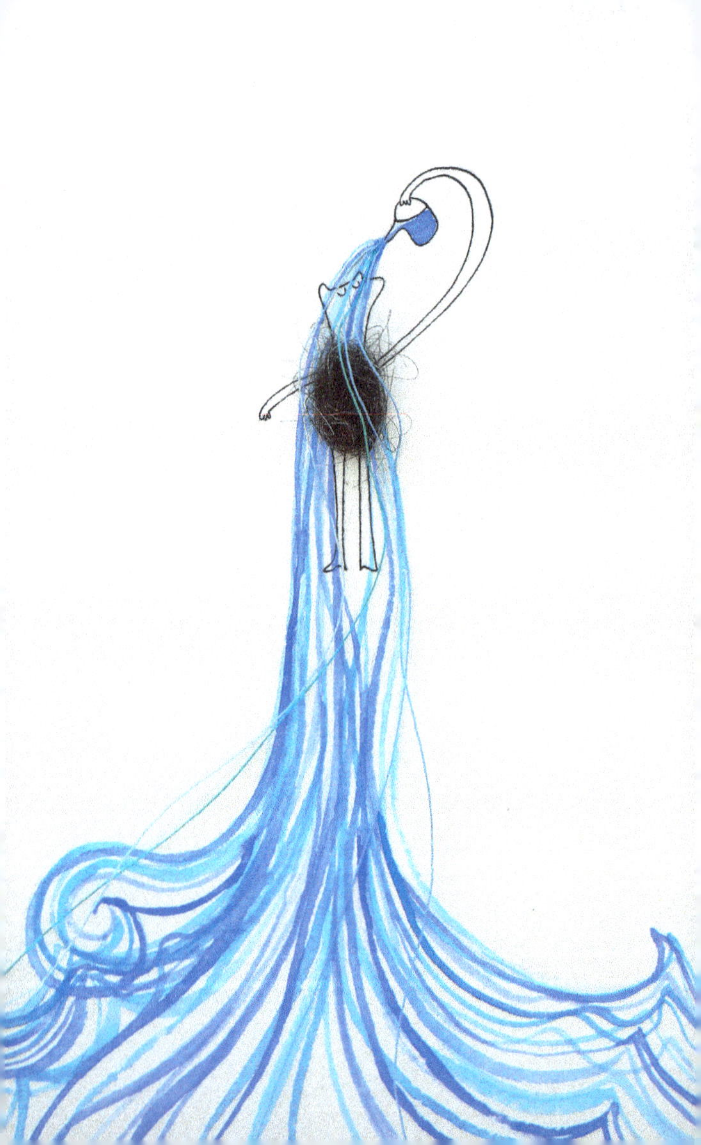

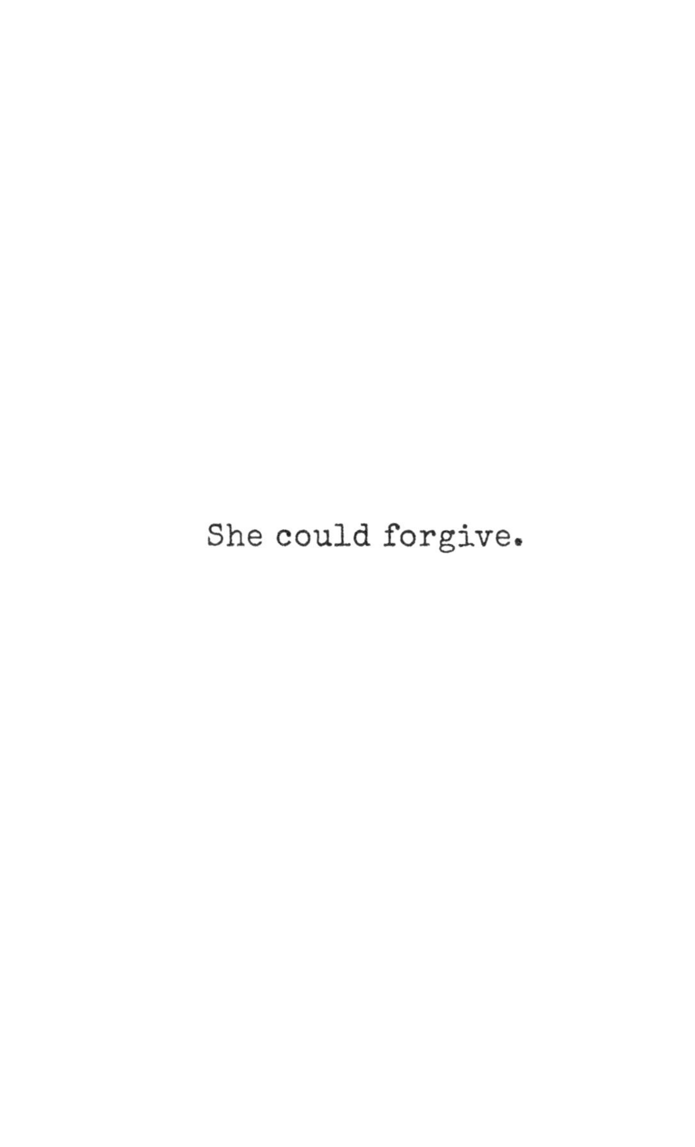
She could forgive.

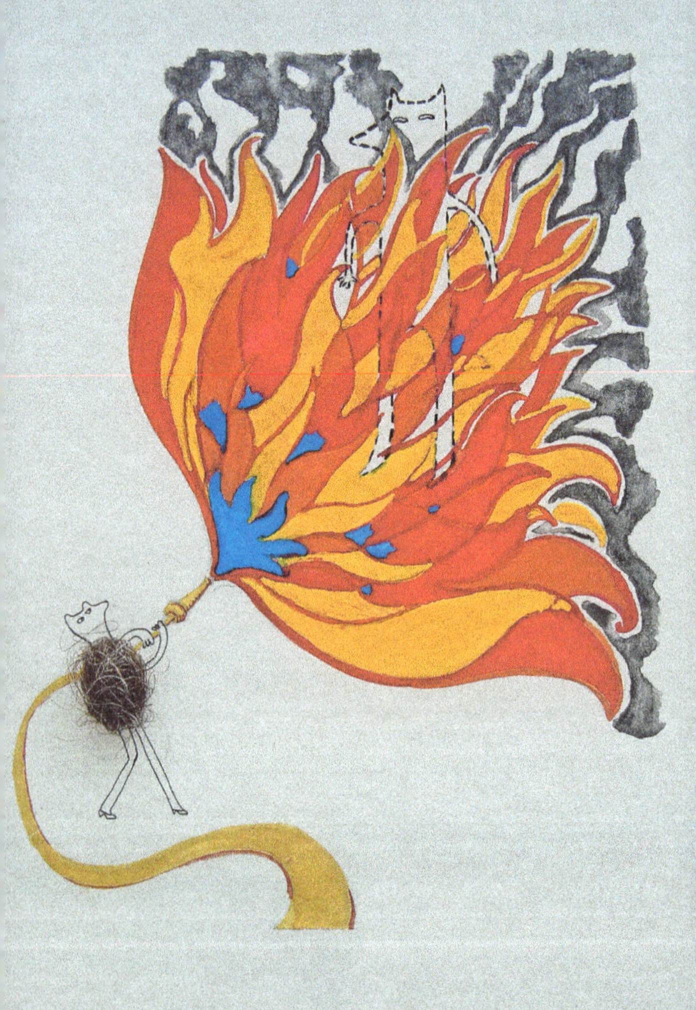

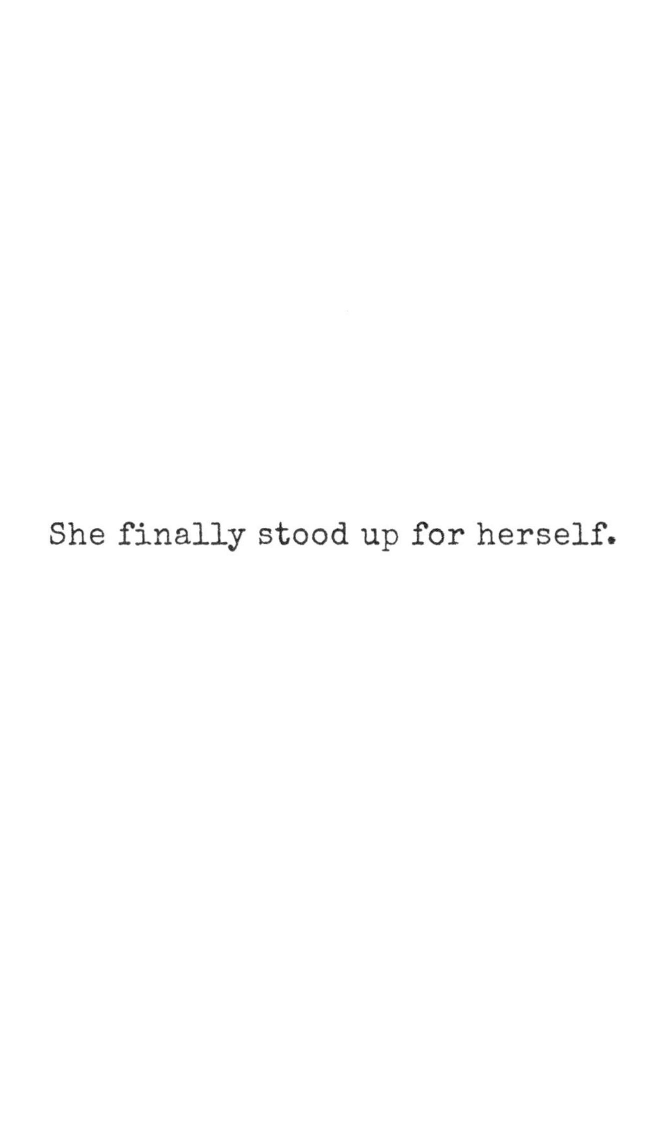

She finally stood up for herself.

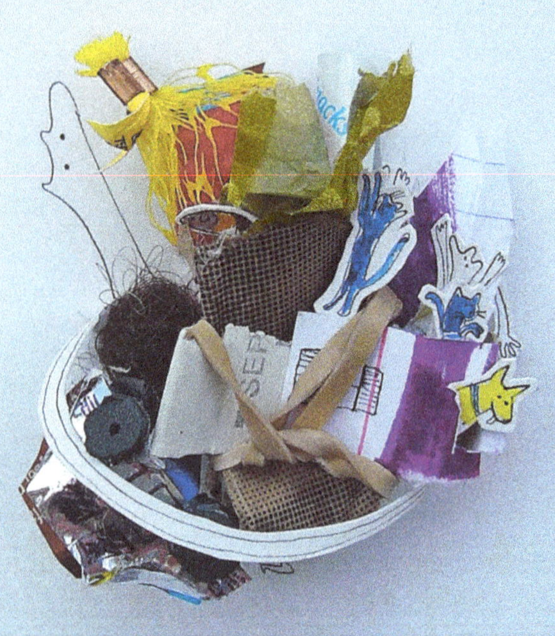

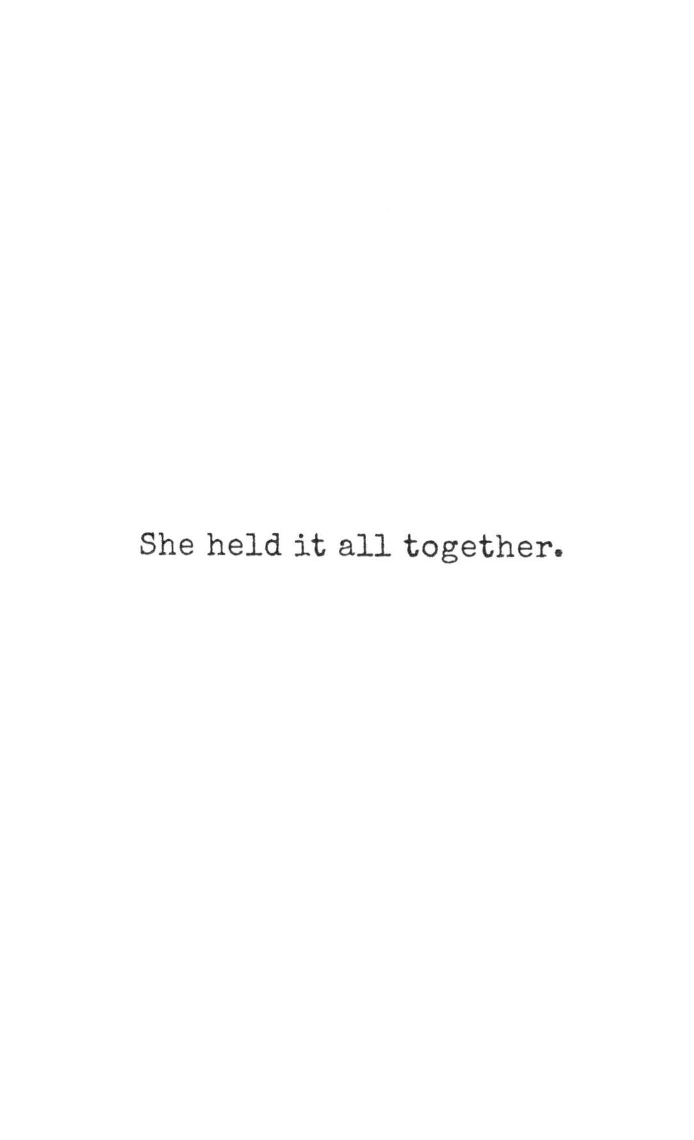

She held it all together.

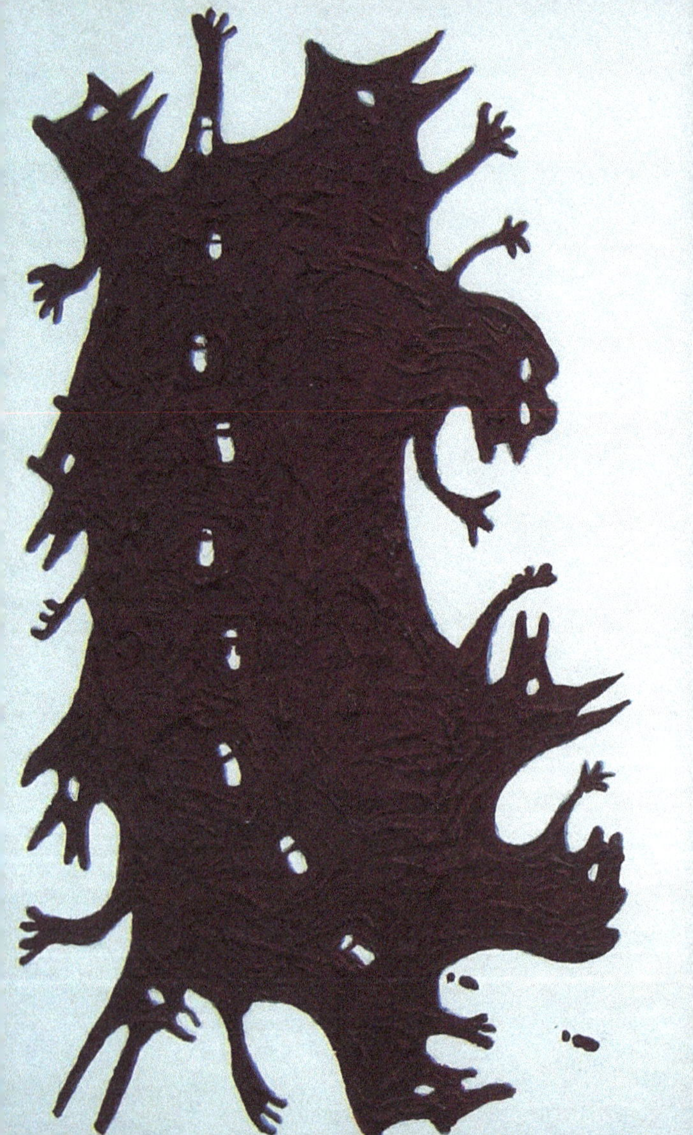

She was the strong one.

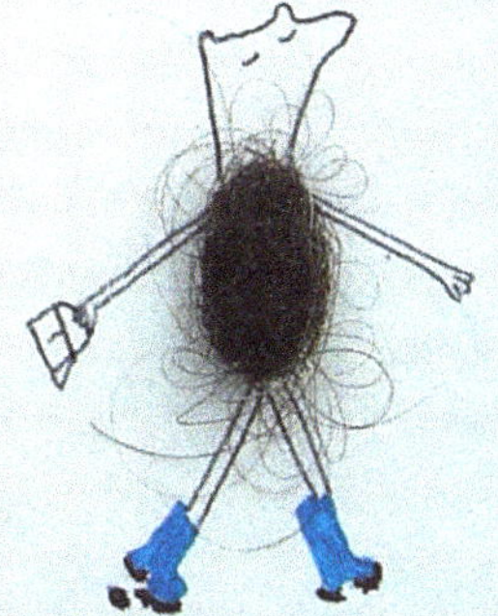

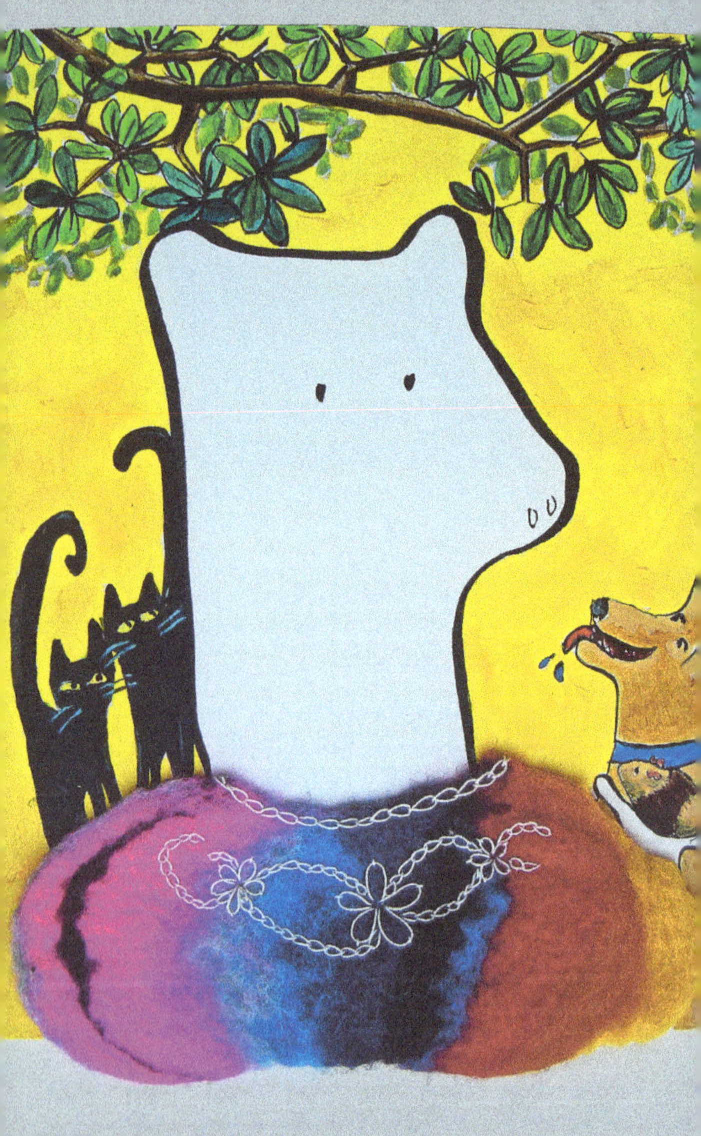

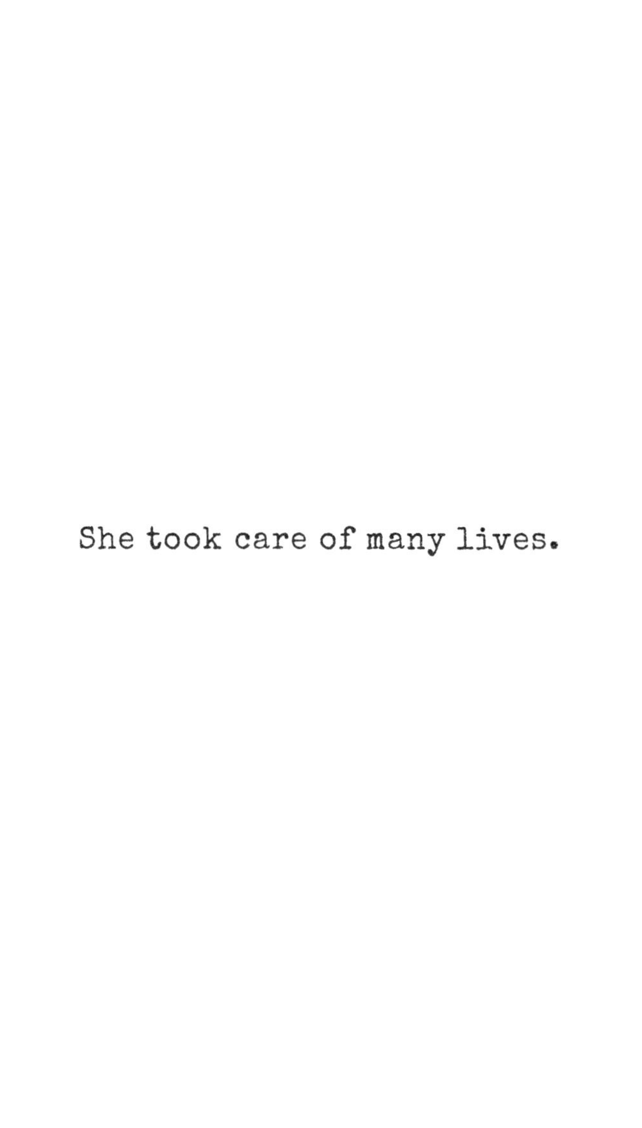

She took care of many lives.

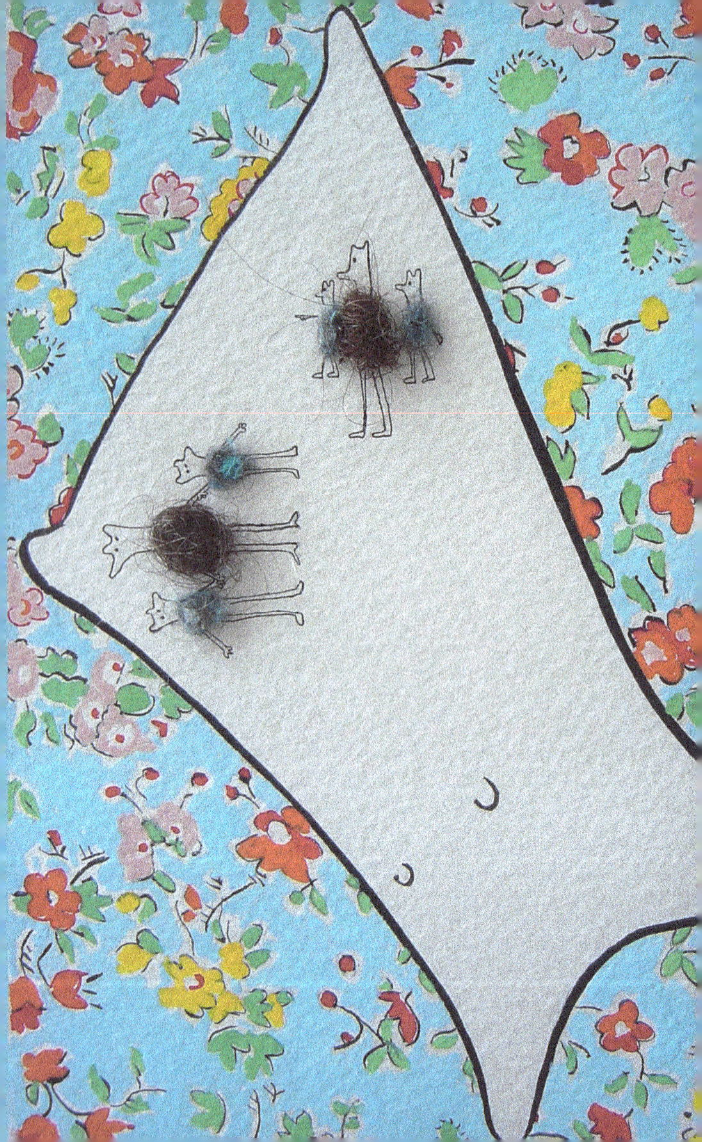

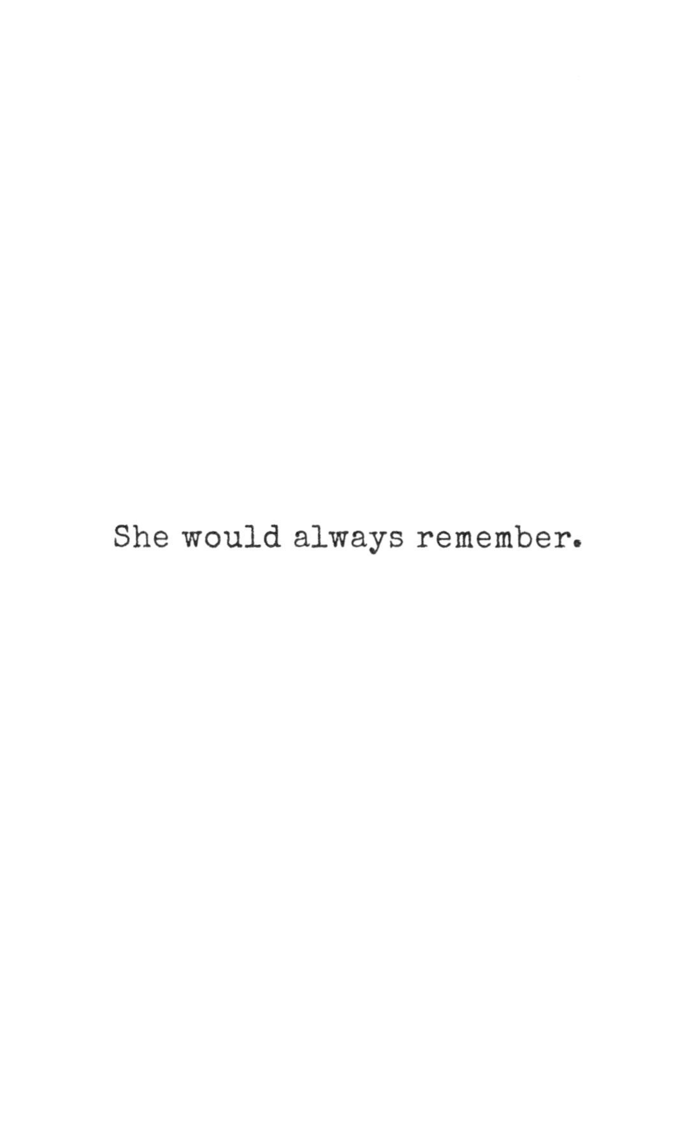
She would always remember.

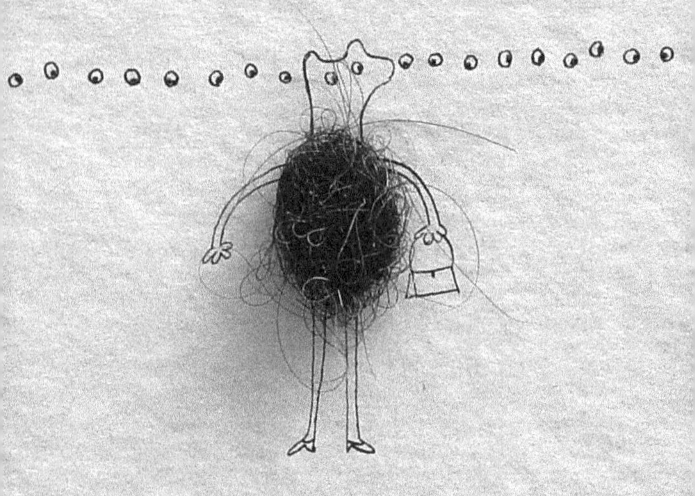

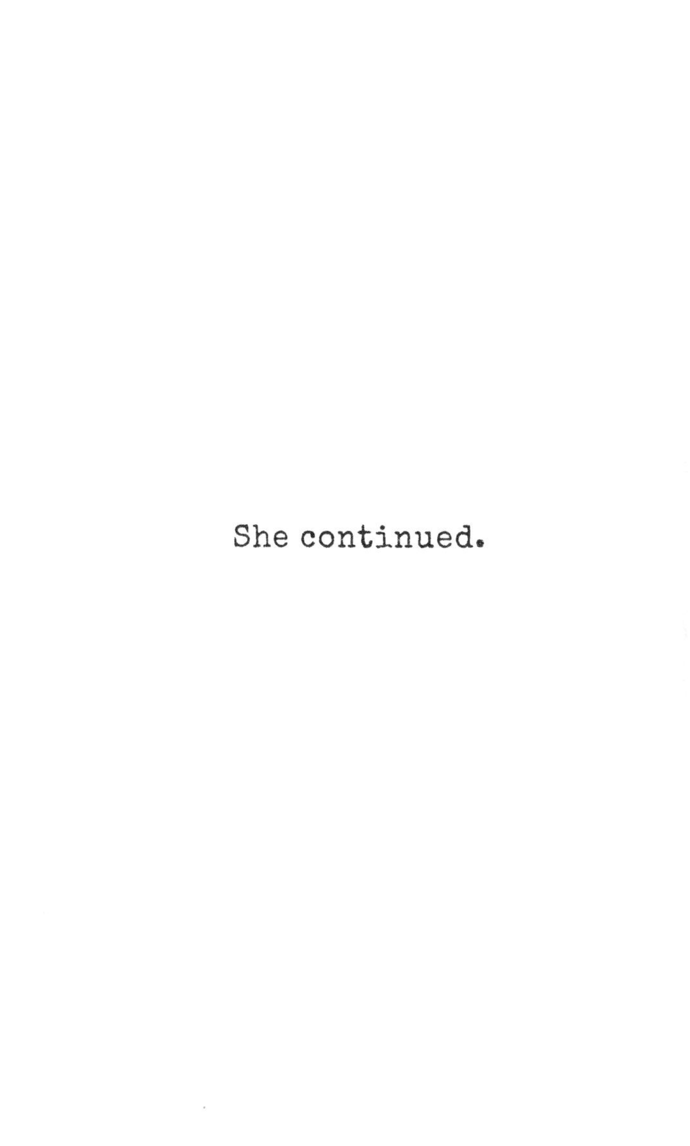

She continued.

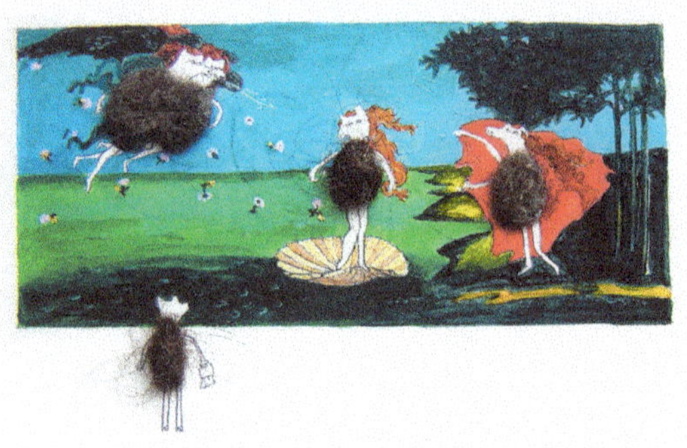

First published in 2019 by Valley Press
Woodend, The Crescent, Scarborough, YO11 2PW
www.valleypressuk.com

ISBN 978-1-908853-95-0
Cat. no. VP0112

Book design by Jamie McGarry.

Printed and bound in Great Britain by
Ashford Colour Press, Gosport.